PHYSICAL EDUCATION IN THE NURSERY AND INFANT SCHOOL

PHYSICAL EDUCATION IN THE NURSERY AND INFANT SCHOOL

PAULINE WETTON

ROUTLEDGE

First published 1988 by Croom Helm Ltd
Reprinted by Routledge 1990, 1991, 1992, 1993, 1996
11 New Fetter Lane, London EC4P 4EE

© 1988 Pauline Wetton

Printed and bound in Great Britain by
Mackays of Chatham PLC, Chatham, Kent

British Library Cataloguing in Publication Data

Wetton, Pauline
  Physical education in the nursery and
  infant school.
  1. Physical education for children
  I. Title
  372.8'6044   GV443

  ISBN 0-415-00543-4

Contents

Introduction

The purpose of this book is to provide a text for students on initial teacher training courses and for those teachers of young children who have requested some guidelines in the teaching of physical education in pre-school play groups, nursery schools and infant schools. Information is given about the physical education curriculum based on the needs of children aged between three and seven. Guidance is given on the selection of activities and methods for the different age levels and lesson plans are suggested.

One particular area of concern for teachers seems to be how to achieve progression in their work and I have therefore attempted to give details of activities in order of difficulty so that teachers can plan their work accordingly. I have also suggested both weekly and yearly programmes to give teachers some help in achieving a long-term perspective.

However, it must be emphasised that any attempt to classify work in stages is only for convenience, as children mature at widely varying rates. This maturation is a result of many circumstances ranging from individual physical differences to diverse environmental backgrounds. It is obvious, for instance, that a four year old from a secure family on a garden housing estate will need a different starting point than a four year old who lives in a high-rise flat in a socially deprived area. But since both children come under the influence of the teacher, then the teacher's role becomes highly significant. Thus one chapter of this book is devoted to the importance of the teacher's role.

Clearly, then, the focus of activity in physical education lessons is the child and the younger the child, the more the teacher, nursery nurse or auxiliary will need to concentrate on personalising and individualising the child's experiences. Consequently, material is offered in Chapters 4, 5 and 6 on the importance of play and the structuring of environments for physical play so that the younger child can be guided into a self-selection learning approach to the development of motor skills. However, the author firmly believes that teachers and assistants should guide children through these learning experiences.

It is also the author's firm belief that fitness activities must be included in the curriculum. This statement may make some educators recoil with horror, but it is increasingly evident that many of our younger children are not physically fit. Research is also showing that it is important to establish patterns of activity during the early years to avoid the development of unhealthy patterns of inactivity. In other words, we need to break the TV syndrome. If we can instil positive attitudes about activity, an understanding of the effects of fitness in children and encourage a physically active day, then we may be able to re-awaken children's awareness of the joy of physical play.

Local Education authorities are currently responding to a DES report (Warnock, 1978) and also to the 1981 Education Act, which legislates for certain children who might formerly have been classified as children needing education in a special school, to be moved into mainstream education. There are separate texts that cover the physical education needs of the children who will remain in special schools and also specialists who are better qualified than the author who can comment on integrating children with special needs into mainstream education. The chapter on children with special needs is, therefore, seen as a guide to teachers in the initial stages of integrating these children into mainstream schools.

Throughout this book I have emphasised a broad approach to the teaching of physical education as I believe that young children need exposure to many movement activities if they are to develop fully and individually. A broad programme gives children a chance to find success and meaning in activity and since it is widely accepted that the younger the child, the more he learns through physical activity, then it is of vital importance to analyse his educational environment and to be aware of the many concepts that can be learned, reinforced and illustrated through physical activity within the physical education programme.

1

Curriculum and Planning

There are several important considerations that must be taken into account when establishing an educationally sound curriculum for physical education. The most crucial one is that the curriculum should be structured as an integral part of the total school curriculum and should reflect the schools' philosophy about their particular children's needs and the ways in which their own children learn. It is important to go beyond the general and sometimes clichéd statement, that the aims of physical education are the same as those of general education — that we are trying to ensure the greatest development of each child as an individual and that we are trying to prepare that child to take his place as a citizen in a democratic society. We all know that we are working towards the development of the whole person physically, socially, emotionally and intellectually, but it is important to think about how this can be achieved. Undoubtedly, physical education can make a significant contribution to the child's total development, physical development, physical fitness and the development of the concept of 'self'.

The first consideration then, when planning the curriculum of any educational establishment is to take careful account of the needs of the children. Initially, it is important to look at the environment in which the children live and also to look at the background against which the school life is set. A child, for example, who lives in a high-rise inner-city flat will probably need more access to play in the nursery and more outdoor PE lessons in the infant school than a child who lives in a cottage in the country. It is also possible that a child who lives in a socially deprived area may need a different programme from one who lives in an upper middle-class area. Clearly, it is necessary for each school to identify the characteristics, the interests and the motivating drives of children from these differing environments.

1

Age, too, will play a part in the identification of needs, although maturational level, physique and physical fitness may be more important factors at the pre-school stage.

The following are suggested guidelines to be used when constructing a PE curriculum:

1.   The curriculum should give direction to the programme and should be written in sufficient detail for each year group to ensure that activities are taught in a sequential manner.

2.   The material should be selected from a wide variety of activities using different teaching methods so that each child experiences success.

3.   The choice of activities should be based on sound educational principles and should offer something for all the children, regardless of their present skills.

4.   Practical work should contain both vigorous activity and movement training, together with time for creativity, repetition and controlled free play.

5.   The weather could affect programme planning and is an important consideration in the balance of a young child's day. For example, prolonged periods of inclement weather (rain or snow) could result in an alteration to the programme. Outdoor lessons would need to be brought indoors and where playtime is not possible, then additional physical activities would need to be provided.

6.   Allowance should be made for thematic work that the teacher may wish to integrate into the physical activity sessions.

7.   Children's special interests should be included as and when they arise.

8.   The written detail should not restrict the teacher and her class, but should be regarded as a guide to lead her to the objectives of the programme and thus ensure progress.

9.   Teachers should be aware of the language that can be acquired, repeated and assimilated whilst children are taking part in PE activities.

10.   Teachers should also be aware of number concepts that can be reinforced in these activities.

However, the specific objectives of any PE curriculum should have a similar basis regardless of the geographical or environmental location of the school. These objectives are:

1.   To develop levels of personal fitness.
2.   To advance physical skills.

3. To promote physical growth.

4. To develop competency in movement.

5. To provide stimulating environments so that children can be creative, use their natural play instincts and release pent-up energy.

6. To guide play behaviour in social situations into desirable experiences.

7. To assist in the development of verbal and non-verbal communication.

8. To assist in the development of conceptual skills and cognitive awareness.

9. To help the children to develop self-concept and to be secure, happy and confident in life situations.

Planning to achieve these stated objectives requires considerable powers of observation and evaluation on the part of the teacher and ways to achieve this are discussed fully in Chapter 2.

However, it is possible to make a general statement about planning and I have divided this into two sections — pre-school and infant school.

PRE-SCHOOL

Pre-school play groups, nursery schools and nursery classes are all included in this section since even though each of these three kinds of establishment can be structured differently, they should have identical basic provision for young children. This basic provision should include the following:

1. Free choice of access to a physical play environment.
2. Locomotor and gross motor experiences.
3. Fine motor and manipulative experiences.
4. Group activities with the teacher.

1. There should be free access to physical play both indoors and outdoors (except in exceptionally bad weather) for all children during the free choice periods within the establishment. This physical play can be sub-divided into the following activities: locomotor, gross motor, fine motor and manipulative. It should be possible to experience physical play on a self-selection basis. Opportunities should be provided for the children to explore, try out, practise, consolidate and create their own movement patterns within an environment

3

structured by the teacher. It is during this kind of play that the teacher can choose to intervene should she see an opportunity to advance the children's learning. For child-selected play activities, children should be exposed to the following experiences.

2. Locomotor and gross motor experiences, which include climbing up, along, over, under and through large pieces of apparatus; also, pushing, pulling, running, walking, balancing, jumping, crawling, carrying, throwing, lifting, riding equipment with wheels, building with large blocks, planks, etc. and 'rough-and-tumble'.

3. Fine motor and manipulative experiences include hammering, sawing, tying, zipping, pressing, cutting, inserting, pouring, holding, twisting and turning — hand activities, together with the use of crayons, brushes, chalks, etc. and modelling clay, plasticine, etc.

4. The teacher should, however, also organise group activities and occasionally, particularly for expressive activities, class activities in the following areas: rhythmic activities, including action songs and rhymes and also, dancing; expressive activities — movement based on selected themes or make-believe ideas; health-related fitness (see Chapter 3); special group activities (see Chapter 7); activities for three year olds and four year olds and games that involve practice in locomotor and manipulative skills. Table 1.1 illustrates a weekly plan that might be followed.

Table 1.1: A suggested weekly plan for teacher-directed activities

MONDAY	Rhythmic activity	10 mins
	Special group x 2	10 mins
	Games activities	5 mins (outdoors)
TUESDAY	Expressive activity	10 mins
	Health-related fitness	10 mins
WEDNESDAY	Rhythmic activity	10 mins
	Special group x 2	10 mins
	Games activities	10 mins (outdoors)
THURSDAY	Expressive activities	10 mins
	Health-related fitness	10 mins
FRIDAY	Expressive or rhythmic activities	10 mins
	Health-related fitness activity	10 mins
	Special groups	10 mins

A lesson plan for a group activity might be structured as follows:

Introduction

'I am going outside to play some games, you can join me if you like', or 'All the four-year-old children follow me!'

Warm-up

'Run anywhere you like, when I clap my hands come and sit by me' (4 repetitions) followed by 'Stretch as tall as you can, now curl up as small as you can' (3–4 repetitions).

Learning skills

'Walk carefully and when I say "stop" stand very still and do not wobble', followed by 'Walk slowly and when I say "now" try and stand on one leg'.

Game

'What time is it Mr Wolf?'

Each group activity should have a purpose and should be constructed with the following questions in mind:

1. Why am I doing this? What are the children learning?
2. Have I included some warm-up activities?
3. Have I built on the material I presented last time?
4. Are the children being given a new learning situation?
5. How can I structure a game situation in which the children can use the skills already practised?

Sometimes during the year it may be necessary to alter this weekly schedule for a variety of reasons such as a special visit, or because of good or bad weather conditions. It is particularly important to extend the teacher-directed activities on days when children cannot have free access to the outdoor play area because of severe weather conditions. Most children have a need to run and exercise freely and when this is denied them they can become frustrated. On the other hand, during periods of warm weather the programme cane be supplemented by extra teacher-directed activities outdoors. Many pre-school leaders, for instance, arrange special 'water' sessions during the summer months. The children often have the pleasure of paddling in an inflatable paddling pool, or have fun with a hose pipe. Sometimes plastic baby baths are used. This kind of controlled water play with an adult is a good way of helping children to understand the properties of water and will help give them confidence when they go to the swimming pool. It is a very important first stage in teaching children to swim — making them 'water happy!'

So that all this material is covered, there needs to be a written syllabus that lists and gives details of the learning experiences to which pre-school children will be exposed and some recognition of the fact that there will be, or should be, a difference in the activities of three-year-old children and those who have been in the nursery school for one year already. In view of the importance of helping children with special needs, written material with suggestions for providing activities for such children should be available (see Chapter 7).

THE INFANT SCHOOL

Compulsory education begins for this age group and this can make a difference to the planning of the curriculum. However, generally speaking, there should be at least one period of teacher-structured physical education each day. The periods or lessons should be selected from the following areas — large apparatus work, small apparatus work, gymnastic floorwork, movement connected with thematic work in the classroom, movement with music, including rhythmic work, swimming, games activities, and folk dancing. In addition, children should have access, in the classroom, to the following items and activities, depending on their age and level of maturity — large building blocks, toys with wheels for pushing, pulling and riding, dressing-up clothes, opportunities for cutting, pouring, holding and carrying items, twisting and turning things, using crayons, brushes, chalk, etc., modelling clay, etc., hammering, sawing and pressing items and finally, teacher-directed action songs and rhymes.

Children who have not had experience of either pre-school play group or nursery education will need special consideration as it is possible that they have not had access to the wide variety of physical learning experiences that the other children have enjoyed. The teacher will need to be very perceptive and may need to guide individual children to activities which will help them advance their physical skills. Patience is also needed as these children will require time to explore, to make mistakes and to master new skills. Hence there is a necessity, particularly in reception classes, to have some of the same facilities that are provided in nurseries and play groups. Schools might, for instance, consider providing a climbing frame with a slide indoors, or better still, free access to a playground outside.

The length of PE lessons in the infant school should vary depending on the age of the children, i.e. reception classes might have 15 minutes of movement with music whereas top infant classes might have 30 minutes. Teachers should be allowed flexibility in timing their lessons, provided that the sanctity of hall-timetabling is not abused! Similarly, some reception-class children in certain environments might need two periods of PE per day, one indoors and one outdoors, or perhaps two lessons outdoors, particularly where free access to outdoor play is not possible.

The weekly programme will vary therefore, depending on the children's backgrounds, on whether they are in reception class or middle or top infant classes, or whether the school is organised into year-band groupings, vertical groupings or, as in the case of village schools, all-age groupings. Broadly speaking then, there should be, in any given week and over any particular year:

1. Activity which involves locomotor and gross motor development.
2. Activity which involves fine motor development.
3. Activity which involves moving rhythmically in a dance form.
4. Activity which encourages physical fitness.
5. (Ideally) activity in water.

These five areas can be explored through any of the mediums listed on p. 3.

Where age-group banding is the norm, activities should be listed in sequential order for each age group so that skill can be acquired. The learning situation should be structured so that progression can be achieved. Furthermore, in order to facilitate this progression, a teacher should be prepared to communicate with the teacher taking the class the following year in order that she is aware of the stage the children have reached, so that continuity and progression is ensured.

It is important to plan the year's programme so that all the activities which a school staff wish to include in the curriculum are taught. If there is no plan or syllabus, then learning can become very haphazard and important activities could be neglected. Because of the lack of facilities available in certain schools, it might be necessary for teachers to plan ahead the activities that can only take place in the summer months and require, for example, access to an outdoor grassed area or access to a swimming pool.

Structure, progression and the acquisition of skill are also more likely to occur if each teacher keeps a note of the material, taken from the syllabus, which has been covered in each lesson. The teacher who has planned her lesson is much more likely to have decided on a purpose or an objective for the lesson and is therefore more likely to teach and keep to her desired objective. These notes can be referred to on a daily, weekly, monthly or yearly basis and an effective evaluation can be made.

Finally, each lesson should be planned under the following headings — aim, introduction, skill learning or movement training, game or dance or practice and closing activity.

Introduction

Any relevant activity that creates a slow build-up to energetic activity. The movements should be easy so that an effort is made to increase the rate of heartbeat and the breathing rate without undue stress.

Skill learning or movement training

This is the time in the lesson to present new learning experiences and to allow repetition of known skills. This is the moment when the teacher should attempt to teach the class a new skill or movement or should attempt to present an aesthetic experience.

Game, dance, practice

A framework should be presented in which children can experience and use the skills already acquired, or can practise those skills which have just been introduced. It should be an enjoyable, structured, play situation.

Closing activity

This can be any relevant activity that calms the class and enables the teacher to create a quiet transition back into the classroom. Alternatively, if the lesson is taking place in the classroom, it can be a transitional, quiet activity to take the children on to their next learning experience.

In conclusion, to create an effective curriculum for younger children, it is critically important for staff within schools to be prepared to sit down together and to be willing to state their aims and objectives for physical education, to write out a syllabus for physical education and to prepare their lessons from this syllabus. Furthermore, they should be prepared to teach in a systematic manner. In so doing, they will have an effective reply to a recent statement:

There was little evidence of the progressive acquisition of skills. One factor which appeared to lead to work of high quality and progression was the presence of supportive and effective guidelines.

Education 5 to 9: An illustrative survey of 80 First Schools in England (HMI, 1982).

2

The Role of the Teacher

The teacher's role is complex. She is responsible for selecting a sound, well-balanced programme of activities and for creating an environment where progressive learning can take place. She is also the director, manager, facilitator and evaluator of her children's learning.

This chapter offers specific advice on how the teacher's role evolves. It explores the planning, management and knowledge needed if the teacher's role is to be effective. It also tackles the crucial notions of evaluation and assessment and suggests practical guidelines by which teachers can observe children's physical development. It highlights the importance of good communication and discipline and links this with the positive procedures needed to make the environment safe for both children and teacher to work in. Finally, there are suggestions about how PE copes with contemporary issues such as moral development, sexism and racism.

PLANNING

The responsibility of the teacher begins with a commitment to the long-term planning of the curriculum so that not only is a syllabus for physical education formulated, but effective cross-curricular links are made. Other subject specialists[1-3] have produced texts that indicate how physical activities can be used to extend and reinforce children's understanding of scientific, mathematical and linguistic concepts during physical activities and scheduled physical-education lessons both in infant schools and in the pre-school establishments. In order to be effective in PE, teachers should be aware of how these cross-curricular ideas and projects can be used to best advantage. The quality of the children's learning could be affected if the teacher is not prepared to make plans in advance, to research and to organise her material sequentially.

Since the role of the teacher is also to help children develop socially and emotionally as well as intellectually and physically, both long-term and short-term planning should take account of these two important aspects of children's development. For instance, many children entering pre-school or infant school will be experiencing their first social contacts outside the family context. For some children, it will be their first experience of co-operating with children who do not speak their language or understand their culture. For others, it will be their first experience of meeting children with special needs. Almost all the children will be beginning a process of institutionalisation not known to them before.

It is the teacher's role, therefore, to consider which aspects of the PE curriculum can best provide opportunities for the children to learn to work and play together co-operatively. She must ensure that the shy child can also learn to interact with others. She must also try to provide experiences which will help all the children to respect the rights of others and understand their feelings. Many traditional physical education activities such as ball play and climbing will create both social and physical opportunities to help the teacher to engineer social interaction as will 'rough-and-tumble' play, home-corner play and building with large blocks. The teacher's responsibility is to consider which physical activities should be offered in order to satisfy her own children's needs.

The role of the pre-school teacher[4] is slightly different from that of the infant-school teacher in this respect. On the whole, in pre-schools, the accepted philosophy is that children will generally be allowed to become independent and self-directed in their learning, whilst in infant schools, because of the nature of the environment, the children's learning will be guided and often directed by the teacher. Children in pre-schools have a less formal environment in which interactions with their peers can be tentatively explored without conflict and where there are more adults to intervene and ease the children from child centredness into more acceptable social patterns. The pre-school environment is structured so that children can learn through physical play of their own choice and through such play, gain many opportunities to enhance social awareness.

The infant teacher has, by design, a much more difficult task than the pre-school teacher, for example, traditionalists often favour the more direct teaching of the three Rs from an early age. Such strategies often result in teaching methods that allow little scope for children

11

to learn through physical activities. It could be argued that unless the teacher plans very carefully and very specifically, children's social, emotional, physical and intellectual development will suffer. Everyone acknowledges the importance of children being literate and numerate; but there are other educational aims that also have value. The teacher must, for instance, have concern for the building of her children's characters, for helping them to integrate socially, for helping them to develop their creative powers, for encouraging them to be independent learners, for helping them to understand the need for a healthy lifestyle and for helping them to cope emotionally with all the new and profound learning expected of them. Early childhood educators who forget that children learn through play — by using their bodies, are creating environments that do not fulfil the needs of any child, whatever their race, creed or culture!

Teachers must also plan for the emotional needs of children. There is a body of research [5-9] that shows quite clearly that bodily activity is necessary both to fulfil children's innermost needs and to create emotional stability. This kind of bodily play may be categorised as follows:

1. Functional play.
2. Purposeless play — 'letting-off steam', 'rough-and-tumble'.
3. Temper or aggressive display.
4. Dramatic play.
5. Rhythmic play.

1. Functional play is the kind of play in which the youngest pre-school child may become involved and also children who are physically and/or mentally retarded. It is in this kind of play that children try out the capacities of their own bodies to move objects and to repeat actions and movements which they have carried out many, many times before. Hammering, driving a toy car, bicycling and sliding would all be examples of this kind of bodily play.

2. Rough-and-tumble[10] is bodily activity that appears to have no aim or purpose. It takes the form of intense muscular activity resulting from a need to release charged emotions. This pent-up energy and emotion has two main channels of release, one being vigorous activity and the other, often manifested as many of us know, in loud noise!

3. Aggressive play is the kind of bodily activity that tends to be displayed by a minority of children. For these children, it is an emotional and social problem which shows itself in aggressive behaviour. The teacher's role must therefore be to plan to help these children to develop self-control. This can often take as long to achieve as developing motor control. There are many ways to turn negative behaviour into positive behaviour. One way to help a child to calm down is to provide acceptable physical outlets for aggression, such as pounding plasticine, or banging with a wooden mallet, or opening the door and letting him stamp and shout outside or even letting him throw bean bags across the yard!

4. *Dramatic play* — bodily activity is also needed for role play and to act out dramatic situations. This kind of play is closely linked to the time during a child's development when he feels the need to 'dress-up'; the physical activity manifested at this time takes many forms. Usually it shows itself in the form of house-play or life-related play such as keeping a shop, a zoo, a café, etc. The physical and language play associated with this development is known to help children 'play out' emotional problems.

5. *Rhythmic play* — rhythm can be used as a therapeutic tool for all children and in particular, for those with special needs. Usually normal children enjoy action songs and rhymes that give them a chance to experiment with the use of their bodies and with sound to create rhythm. This kind of activity also encourages group co-operation. Other rhythms can be played out on self-selected instruments such as a drum or a tambourine. The sounds the children make and the energy they use will depend on the emotion they wish to express. Movement to musical accompaniment also gives children a chance to move their bodies rhythmically and can be a valuable medium to develop self-expression. Some children value this phenomenon as either a group experience or as an individual experience.

Each of these five categories should be analysed by the teacher and the environment should be modified to allow bodily activity of this nature to take place. Sadly, many pre-school establishments and even more infant schools create the opposite kind of environment. I classify this as the 'Top Shop' mentality! Features of this are where adults place obstacles such as tables or display areas in the children's way or close the doors to the outside so that vigorous play activity cannot take place. This kind of treatment denies the children's need to move. Certain children need this kind of outlet more than others and there is certainly enough research evidence[11-12] now to show that young children, particularly boys, cannot be expected to exist without it. Some pre-school establishments plan the children's day around blocks of time and arrange a time outdoors or a playtime much like an infant school. I would suggest that this is not satisfactory for most children up to the age of six and for some children, never at all!

Many researchers,[13] have observed young children at play in 'free-choice time', and there is clear evidence that if children are allowed to be physically active when the need is felt, rather than at some pre-ordained time, there is a renewed power of concentration on finer motor tasks and more sustained effort in intellectual pursuits.

MANAGEMENT

Having decided on the content of the curriculum and having considered the children's social, emotional, intellectual and physical needs, the teacher's next task is to consider the ways in which she will manage the children both indoors and outdoors. Child management is, for most people, a skill which develops gradually and which must have constant appraisal and evaluation. As a teacher's management skill develops, it gradually evolves into a mode of working which frequently becomes highly personal and idiosyncratic. It is often identified as a teaching style of working and incorporates many facets of behaviour of which class management is just one. There are many different teaching styles. Some teachers may have an energetic extrovert style, others may have a quiet style, some a happy or comic style, all of which can be successful in managing children. Central to all these styles however, is usually, a sympathetic teacher, one who likes and respects the children and is willing to really listen to them, who knows how to stimulate them to develop their potential, and lastly, one who knows when to encourage, when to challenge, when to chastise gently and when to praise.

Knowledge

It seems to follow that a teacher who manages children well will undoubtedly be a better teacher if she is knowledgeable about her subject material. Most people would argue that a teacher of younger children needs a thorough understanding of child development and, within this general framework, a specific knowledge about children's physical growth and motor development. Such areas are well researched and documented in many texts.[14-15] Further to this, the teacher needs access to specific physical education activities in the areas of dance, gymnastics (large apparatus), games (small apparatus) and swimming. Most adults working in establishments with young children, where successful learning takes place, share their knowledge about physical education and create both a common philosophy and common guidelines for the curriculum. The 'team' should constantly review the guidelines in the light of any new literature, research, or DES publications that become available. In addition, in-service training courses are a very valuable source of new ideas and provide a platform for discussion about the current use of materials. The Physical Education Association of Great Britain and Northern Ireland[16] is another source of information.

Methods

The methods which a teacher can use to pass on the information which she wishes the children to learn are very varied. In order to ensure that learning takes place, a teacher can select one or many methods, or can mix methodologies (even within a single lesson). Some methods, for instance, may be more suitable and productive for a certain age group and for certain kinds of material, whilst other methods may be more useful to fulfil certain objectives. An exploratory approach may be far more suitable for the younger child, for a child deprived of play or for introducing any child to new apparatus, than a direct approach. Five methods are suggested here:

1. Exploratory — when using the exploratory method in PE, the teacher provides the children with a learning environment (pre-school) or a large apparatus layout (infant school), or an object such as a ball, bat, or tambourine and allows the children to experiment and to play in order to begin to understand the potential of the apparatus, and become 'movement happy' on it or with it.

2. Task-orientated — in this method, the teacher sets a task and the children are requested to respond by moving in different ways. The children are challenged to find their own way of using their bodies to answer the task. This allows children to be creative and to work at their own individual level. Such a task might be 'Show me how you can move along the floor on one foot and one hand', or 'Show me how you can move about on two feet and two hands.'

3. Problem-solving — here the teacher sets an open-ended problem which allows the children to respond with one or many answers. This method encourages exploration and practice and should produce a wide variety of movements in the children's responses. The challenge is once again issued in the form of a command, e.g. 'Find a way of moving along near to the floor', or 'Listen to the sound and think of different ways of moving to it.' It goes without saying that the problems must be geared to the skill level of the children and their conceptual understanding.

4. *Guided discovery* — in this method, the teacher knows the skill that she wants the children to learn but, through her shrewd guidance, the children appear both to discover and to learn the skill for themselves. A feature of such a mode of working is that there is more teacher involvement than there might appear to be. A simple example might illustrate the point — learning to catch. The teacher suggests various strategies, the children try them, talk to the teacher about them and finally arrive at a skilful performance. The teacher tells the children to find a partner and:

1. Throw and catch a big ball.
2. Hold your hands out to catch the ball.
3. Keep your feet together.
4. Keep your feet apart.
5. Be ready to move your feet.

The children arrive at a satisfactory solution by talking to the teacher about the tasks they have been set. 'I need to move my feet', 'The ball bounces off my hands if I hold them like that, what should I do?', etc.

5. *Direct or Instructional Approach* — certain skills, however, require a much more direct teaching method. The more precise the skill to be assimilated, the more this method must be used. Sometimes, a direct method is needed for a number of reasons:

1. To prevent an injury. When teaching, for example, the forward roll, the importance of tucking in the head should be emphasised.
2. To complete the skill succesfully. For example, the hand and arm position for headstand and handstand should be pointed out.
3. To re-teach a skill which is being performed wrongly. For example, placing the left hand above the right hand when holding a cricket bat (for a right-handed child).
4. To introduce a lesson.
5. To control a class of difficult children.
6. To vary the methodology.
7. To teach fitness exercises.
8. Because the teacher finds the method the most satisfactory for her and her children.

EVALUATION AND ASSESSMENT

Once the teacher has decided on her aims, planned the curriculum according to the children's needs and decided on methodologies, she has the important role of evaluating and assessing both her own and her children's performance.

At the time of writing, certain teachers are showing anxiety about some of the guidelines suggested in the 5–16 curriculum documents,[17] especially where specific standards may have been suggested for particular age groups. One reason for this might be because teachers think that teaching will become target-orientated. It is feared, for example, that instead of assessment being used to produce useful information about children's development and performance, it might be used to determine what is taught. Enlightened teachers worry that if standards are declared, they may be restricted to teaching certain skills and as a result, creative and flexible teaching methods will disappear. I do not think this is necessarily the case. A teacher who is confident and competent in the methods she uses and the material she teaches will not only reach, but may even surpass, any suggested standards laid down in guidelines. On the other hand, it could be argued, that any standards are better than none! At the present time, for instance, we do not have any national standards for physical education, despite the fact that many teachers constantly ask the question 'what should children be able to achieve in PE when they are five, six or seven?'

The unfortunate aspect of standardisation is that only certain skills are able to be tested and that, as has happened in some other areas of the curriculum, teachers might teach to the tests. An even worse scenario might exist where valuable teaching and learning time is used in the individual testing of a child's performance. In my view, methods of assessment should be selected which enable children to be assessed without seriously interrupting the children's physical education programme. Teachers can probably become quite adept at this, since the key to teaching physical education, more than many other aspects of the curriculum, relies on keen observation by the teacher. There are no paintings or writing to assess at leisure. In physical education, there are only quick sequences of movement to be observed and accurate visual judgements to be made and then stored mentally for instant or future reference. Similarly, in the pre-school situation it seems that children are constantly on the move, and again, information must usually be stored in the memory to be recalled at a later date. One could argue that it would take days to catalogue the developmental changes which take place in children in the period between the age of three and entry to school and similarly between school entry and the age of seven. What I would suggest is that not only do teachers and assistants need a framework which will allow them to observe more perceptively, but also they need some easy method of recording the information they gather.

In the pre-school situation, it is possible that the children can be assessed whilst they are busy in free-play periods. All assessors should be encouraged to use this strategy, since it should provide a more naturalistic result. There are several texts [18-19] available which are designed solely to help pre-school personnel obtain a clearer picture of successive stages of development of the children in their care. Most of the tests of physical skills discussed in these texts rely on the teachers using a direct or instructional method but can be incorporated into working in small groups. However, there are no universal tests for infant school children and few free-play situations where children can be assessed naturalistically and the adult-child ratio is higher than in nursery school and consequently any tests which are developed for infant children should be simpler to administer.

The essential element in successful and effective assessment of any child's performance in PE is concensus. Where the staff in a school are willing to work together to suggest simple criteria for assessing and recording standards, more effective learning takes place and more progress can be observed.

OBSERVATION

In addition to the usual evaluation and assessment procedures which are necessary in the primary school, the teaching of physical education relies on the teacher's ability to make immediate assessments in each lesson if appropriate learning is to take place. The teacher must therefore learn to be an accurate observer. In order to facilitate this, the infant teacher should be clear about the objectives which she wishes her children to achieve. If she has planned the work carefully and managed the children accordingly, then careful observation of individual performance should lead towards an improvement in standards.

For example, in a task-orientated lesson, the task presented to the children should be accompanied by clear verbal instructions. Then, as the children work on the task, the teacher should move amongst them, observing the activity and analysing the product. She should make sound judgements about whether the work is challenging the children, whether they are working purposefully, whether any of the work could be used to demonstrate a movement to the rest of the class in an effort to improve performance and lastly, she should make judgements about the teaching points she needs to give to improve performance. The good infant teacher should be observing responses from the whole class and from individual children, and be giving help and encouragement. As a consequence of what she sees, she may decide that a general teaching point, an individual demonstration or some timely questioning will help the children to make progress. A good demonstration by a child is one of the most useful visual aids which the teacher can use effectively in her teaching. Demonstrations can be used to reinforce good practice, to clarify or demonstrate a teaching point, to set a problem-solving situation, to widen movement vocabulary or to show children that there are many different ways of solving the same task. The teacher must be careful however, to concentrate on one teaching point at a time and to put the children into action immediately after the demonstration in order to ensure that good practice ensues. There can be no doubt that good standards are usually achieved in physical education if children are given clear, simple instructions followed by opportunities to practise, to receive guidance, to practise again, to receive encouragement and finally, to repeat and repeat the product.

On the other hand, in pre-schools, the general objective is usually to promote children's development by determining their needs and then to follow this up by providing appropriate apparatus and activities to satisfy them. The specific objectives are to provide equipment and activities which promote the learning of large and fine motor skills, to provide opportunities for children to move their bodies in a variety of ways and to assess the needs of individual children and then prepare plans to help all the children to develop.

As an essential pre-requisite, it is important for pre-school teachers to decide which large motor skills the children possess on entering the nursery. In this way, a teacher can assess whether any child needs immediate specific attention. It would not be a case of necessarily singling out the child, but rather providing group activities where all the children can benefit from the practice and where the teacher can also be sure that the child who needs special help can be supervised as he plays with and alongside other children. As a useful checklist, we can expect children to perform the following large motor skills on entry to pre-school. They should be able to:

1. Stand and walk on tiptoe.

2. Stand on one foot when shown an example.
3. Walk up steps with alternate feet.
4. Walk down steps with two feet to a step.
5. Jump from one step (15–20 cms) on to two feet.
6. Run round obstacles and corners.
7. Run round obstacles and corners whilst pushing or pulling large toys.
8. Pick up and carry a large object.
9. Walk forwards and backwards with confidence when hauling large toys.
10. Ride a tricycle using the pedals and steer it round wide corners.
11. Throw a bean bag.
12. Kick a ball with force.
13. Climb up two or three rungs of a climbing frame and climb down with confidence.

After being involved in free-choice activities and in teacher-structured activities for six months, a further assessment should be made to check whether all the children are developing satisfactorily and also to check specifically for improvement in the performance of any special cases identified in the entry assessment.

After six months in pre-school, children should be able to demonstrate that they can:

1. Balance on one foot for six seconds.
2. Stand, walk and run on tiptoe.
3. Walk up and down steps with alternate feet.
4. Pick up and carry a large object.
5. Ride a tricycle and execute sharp U-turns.
6. Walk along a balance beam for two or three steps.
7. Slide down a slide.
8. Run up and down grassy banks without falling.
9. Jump over a low obstacle.
10. Play alongside another child when block-building, during ball play, and when pushing and pulling a car or cart.
11. Move freely to music.
12. Throw a large ball.
13. Catch a bean bag.
14. Climb up and down and on the climbing frame.
15. Initiate their own play on, for example, a rocking horse, see-saw, rocking boat, roundabout.

16. Kick a large ball towards a target.

This second assessment should make it possible to pick out children who have physical problems and to seek help from support agencies with the co-operation and assistance of the parents.

A final assessment can then be made before entry into infant school. At the end of the pre-school experience, children should be able to demonstrate that they can:

1. Balance on either foot for six seconds.
2. Walk up and down stairs easily.
3. Climb, play and execute various movements on the climbing frame.
4. Push a friend in a toy with wheels.
5. Manoeuvre a tricycle with dexterity.
6. Walk along a balance beam for half the distance.
7. Go down the slide in various ways — feet first, on the tummy and on the back.
8. Push and pull toys with wheels up and down slopes.
9. Throw, catch, bounce and kick a large ball.
10. Hit a ball with a bat.
11. Take part in group games.
12. Listen to simple instructions and put them into practice.
13. Interpret movement ideas e.g. 'move like a worm'.
14. Run in a straight line towards a target.

It is not possible to test all the children in a pre-school on one day. It is therefore a good idea to have child profiles prepared so that members of staff can tick or comment on a child's activities whenever they have observed a child. Another way of assessing the children is for one adult to involve a group of children in a few activities, e.g. balancing, ball play, running and to either carry a clipboard or ask another adult to check the children whilst they are in action. A student teacher could be used to good effect here.

COMMUNICATION

A teacher should also concern herself with the way she communicates with the children. In physical education activities, there is frequently just as much non-verbal communication as there is verbal communication. Both modes have an important place in the learning environment.

The following list gives some of the points to remember when communicating with children:

1. Stand where all the children are visible all the time. This usually means positioning yourself around the periphery of the room with your back to the wall.

2. In strong sunlight, position yourself so that you, and not the children, are looking towards the sun.

3. Vary the tone of your voice. Sometimes it is necessary to project the voice across the room to praise a child whilst at other times, a conversational tone can be used. Use the voice to control, calm or interest the children.

4. Use words, phrases and similes that children can understand. Very young children do not yet know some of the words which are in common school usage, such as line, team, partner, etc. and often have no knowledge about how 'to slither (what does it mean?) like a snake' (what is that?); etc.

5. Try to use good grammatical speech.

6. Use sensible language with younger children, e.g. 'jump like a rabbit' not 'jump like a bunny'.

7. Use instructional language to encourage good performance, such as 'I like that jump, you lifted your knees high', not 'Good jump' or 'Good'.

8. Avoid asking questions such as 'Shall we . . .?' or 'Would you like to . . .?' Make statements instead, such as 'We are all going to . . .' Also, try to vary the phraseology.

9. If the class does not respond to an introductory statement, try re-phrasing the statement, particularly in the early stages with a new class. Many words are often used in our language to describe one object and can throw the children into confusion — gym shoe, sand shoe, pump, etc.

10. Remember that young children respond to kindness, firmness and a reasonable code of rules. They do not understand sarcasm, cynicism or ridicule.

11. Do not talk too much! Young children want to move!

12. Tell the children how you feel. 'I really enjoyed working with you today. Thank you!' or 'I was a bit disappointed with you all today. Do you know why?'

DISCIPLINE

Sometimes indiscipline is caused by the teacher. For instance, it is possible to create a negative atmosphere and to teach unsuitable material. So if a lesson or group activity gets out of control, it is a good idea to stop immediately and move into another environment.

Individual children can cause problems and there are a variety of ways in which the teacher can deal with them. Some of them may be dealt with according to the ground rules which the teacher has set up. The children will know that anyone breaking the ground rules will be firmly dealt with. It might be that 'the rule-breaker' is dealt with through another adult such as an auxiliary, who will cope with the child in the way that the school has agreed. Sometimes a child can be made to sit at the edge of the area and be reminded that he can only join in again when he is ready to work properly. Individual misdemeanours should be dealt with promptly and wherever possible, privately. The whole class should never have to suffer because of an individual's misbehaviour. It is a good idea not to use physical education lessons or activities to punish children. Since almost all young children love physical activities, teachers are sometimes guilty of the bad practice of denying them physical education time for misdemeanours committed at other times. In other words, PE is often used as a form of blackmail. This should be regarded as unsound educational practice!

Boisterous and over-energetic boys seem to be a constant problem to early childhood educators, less so to pre-school staff (where the free-choice system usually allows vigorous play outdoors) than to most infant teachers who have suffered a wet playtime! Teachers should probably consider changing the prepared programme to counter this kind of situation. It might also help if the auxiliary can be deployed to assist particularly inexperienced teachers at times like this.

SAFETY

Another important role which a teacher and the staff in a school must undertake is that of a safety officer. We have all become much more safety conscious of late and many LEAs have guidelines that must be strictly adhered to. The following notes are a general guide:

Environment

1. Equipment should be of the correct size and weight for children in pre-schools and infant schools.
2. Ground surfaces should be flat and free from obstacles. Indoor surfaces should be clean.
3. Walls should be free of protrusions, particularly sharp-angled metal protrusions.
4. There should be adequate lighting.
5. There should be enough space for the number of children working.

Teaching

'The prevention of accidents largely depends on the skill, knowledge and example of the teacher, but he will remember always the need to develop a sense of responsibility amongst his pupils and an understanding of the importance of the part they play in ensuring their own safety, and that of their fellows'.[20]

1. A teacher must select the kind of activities and experiences that are appropriate for the age of the children and their level of experience.
2. Adequate warm-up activities must be provided.
3. Children should be made aware of the dangers that might occur, for example, after the instruction 'Jump down onto the mat please, not onto the floor', explain why — 'The mat is soft and flexible and will cushion your landing.' or 'The mat is like your bed at home. It will help you to land without hurting your feet.'
4. If you are teaching a skill, teach it in progressive stages. This in itself is a safety factor, for example, first teach them to land from a self-initiated jump, then to jump from a bench onto a mat and finally, to jump from a low table onto a mat.
5. Make sure the children know the properties of the apparatus they are using, for example, that ropes swing backwards as well as forwards.
6. Children should be made aware of where the piano protrudes into the room or the position of the TV or the music trolley.
7. Children should be trained to share the apparatus. Make 'in-house' rules about how many people can work at one time and

where to go to wait for a turn.

8.   Children should be encouraged to set out and assemble their own apparatus whenever possible so that they are more aware of how to handle it, adjust it and notice if something is wrong.

9.   The teacher should have overall responsibility in checking that the apparatus is properly set up so that the apparatus is stable and there is enough space for children to move around it.

10.   Allow children to talk when they are working. Keep a 'working noise' level.

11.   The class should be silent when asked.

12.   Teach traffic rules in small apparatus lessons, for example, 'Do not collect your ball until I tell you' or '*Walk* back to me.'

Clothing and footwear

1.   Children should wear sensible clothing for physical activities. In pre-schools, parents should be encouraged to send their children in playsuits or track suits rather than in their best shirts or skirts.

2.   Infant-school children should strip down to vest and pants wherever possible.

3.   Pre-school children should be encouraged to wear soft-soled footwear.

4.   Infant school children should have bare feet for all indoor PE lessons and should be encouraged to come to school in soft-soled shoes such as trainers, ready for outdoor lessons. Working barefooted exercises the muscles of the feet in a much more satisfactory way than when toes are cramped inside shoes.

5.   Children should never wear any kind of jewellery, including watches, or any kind of loose clothing, as the articles may get caught on large apparatus and create an accident. Similarly, never let children work indoors in stockinged feet or long trousers since both can cause slipping.

Safety procedures

There has been a sharpening of concern for safety throughout education since the introduction of the Health and Safety at Work Act 1974. Experienced teachers and physical education teachers have long been aware of the need for safe practices, but no matter how well organised or how safety conscious the staff in early childhood

institutions are, there may still be accidents. It is of crucial importance then, that if there is an accident, the adults should have worked
out a plan of campaign beforehand to cope with this. A suggested
format regarding safety codes and a plan of campaign is as follows:

1. Check with the LEA.
2. Talk together as a staff about procedures in an emergency.
3. Identify which staff have a qualification in first aid.
4. Identify an area for administering first aid.
5. Keep a clearly marked (white cross on a green background)
   first aid box in an identified place.
6. Always keep the box in the same place.
7. Keep the box out of the reach of younger children.
8. Keep the box tidy and well-stocked.
9. Replace any used items.

The Health and Safety at Work Executive recommends a list of contents that should be kept in first aid boxes. Most LEAs also have a
recommended list. The box should contain all the recommended items.
The contents should vary in number of course, depending on the
number of children using the premises.

Accidents

1. If an accident does occur, stop whatever is going on, ask the
children to sit quietly and ask one child to go and fetch another
adult. Never leave the scene of the accident.
2. If the injury looks serious, never move the patient.
3. Keep the child warm by covering her with a blanket and stay
with the child.
4. Another adult should ring for an ambulance and also ring the
child's parents. Wherever possible, the parent should accompany
the child to hospital.
5. All accidents must be recorded in the accident book with:

Name, age and address of the child.
Date and time of the accident.
Type of injury.
Details of the action taken.
Details of the accident.

6. There is a legal obligation (Health and Safety at Work Act)[21] to report major accidents directly to the local office of the Health and Safety Executive on form F2508 within seven days of the accident. Check with your LEA about this form.

First aid

First aid is *if in doubt, don't*!

1. First aid is what it says — it is the first step in caring for an accident victim.
2. There should always be at least one member of staff with a first-aid qualification.
3. Try and keep a space set aside for first aid. If this space doubles as a settee in the staff room, then always keep it clear.
4. Carry the child to the settee, clear away all other spectators except for another adult if necessary.
5. Wash your hands before giving any treatment.
6. All treatment should be administered when the patient is either sitting or lying down.
7. Never give medicines or anything by mouth, not even junior Paracetamol, until the child has been checked by a medical practitioner.[22]

Priorities

1. *Breathing*. If a child has stopped breathing, mouth-to-mouth resuscitation must be started *immediately*. All other treatment takes second place. Resuscitation must be continued until the child starts breathing again.
2. *Bleeding*. If bleeding is excessive, control it by direct pressure on the bleeding point. Try and use a sterilised pad, but in an emergency use the thumb and fingers. Raising a limb if this is the site of the bleeding will help reduce the flow of blood (unless the limb is fractured).
3. *Unconsciousness*. When a child is unconscious, make sure that the airways are clear. Check that the tongue has not blocked the throat. Try and place the child in the recovery position if possible.

Other injuries

1. *Broken bones*. Do not attempt to move the child until the injured parts have been supported in a secure position so that they cannot move. *If in doubt — do not touch.*

2.   *Foreign bodies in the eye.* Irrigate with clean cool water. If the object does not remove itself, or if it cannot be removed easily with moistened sterile material, cover the eye and arrange for the child to go to hospital.

3.   *Cuts, grazes, etc.* Clean the wound of all dirt and grit. Cover with a sterilised dressing.[23-24]

Safety of student teachers and other unqualified personnel

1.   Unqualified personnel should never be left completely alone with a group of children when the children are using large apparatus, or at the swimming pool, or when playing vigorous games.

2.   Students on nursery and teaching practice may take lessons or supervise nursery children but should be observed by a qualified member of staff; the 'duty of care' always rests with the qualified staff even when a student is taking her class.

Safety at the swimming pool

New legislation is being recommended and teachers are urgently requested to always check their LEA guidelines before taking children to the swimming pool.

HEALTH

Children at risk as far as their health is concerned can be spotted very easily when they take part in physical activity sessions, particularly in the infant school when they take off their clothes for PE. All teachers should be able to recognise dirty children, battered children and neglected children.

Nowadays, there seem to be more neglected children around than either dirty or battered children. There are many social reasons for this situation such as one-parent families, poor housing conditions, low-income families, unemployed parents, ignorance of child-rearing, etc. all contributing to categories of neglected children. Frequently, neglected children are very quiet and seem unable to play. They are often not accepted by their peers in group situations and are generally introverted. The children in all these categories need help and their cases should be reported to the head-teacher for possible referral.

It is not uncommon at the present time for schools to have been alerted to the health problems of some children before they actually enter school. This is mainly because such children have been identified through the medical and social services. In these situations, the teacher must make herself fully conversant with any case notes and with any recommendations for suitable practices.

Sometimes an observant teacher can identify a health problem that has not been noticed before, particularly when a child is engaged in vigorous physical activity. Common symptoms of health problems may be identified by the following:

1. Unusual fatigue.
2. Blueing of the lips.
3. Clammy skin — sweating.
4. Shakiness after exercise.
5. Dizziness and fainting.

These observations should be reported to the head-teacher for parental and medical referral.

It is the teacher's role too to make children aware of good health practices wherever possible. It is possible, for instance, to include some knowledge about and increase children's understanding of the human body during PE lessons. It is also possible to make the children aware of the conditions which promote healthy growth and development of the body, such as the importance of exercise and of exercise in the fresh air. A teacher can also provide many experiences during PE lessons which will increase the children's capacity to share and co-operate and to become more aware of their own and others' emotions and feelings.[25]

MORAL DEVELOPMENT

Teachers should be aware that physical education, along with other subjects, can be used as a vehicle to promote moral learning. 'For example when children are involved in games making they begin to gain experience about acting within a code of rules and of patterning relationships both in co-operation and competition with them'.[26] For very young children, moral learning can often happen quite spontaneously as part of an active play situation. For instance, the teacher may have to explain to a child why a particular course of action must be taken when a child who has been involved in rough-and-tumble activity knocks into and spoils another child's building play!

RACE AND SEX

The teacher is also charged with the responsibility of ensuring that children receive an equal education both on the grounds of sexual and racial equality. In early childhood situations, children are not separated for physical activities or physical education lessons. Any inequalities, therefore, are likely to arise in specific situations.

In pre-school, because of the boys' need to be involved in vigorous play and because they present themselves to girls as rough and fast-moving, it is possible for girls to be deprived access to toys with wheels, climbing frames and rumpus areas. Strategies should be worked out to ensure that in free-choice play sessions, children are observed at play and access is made available to both sexes.

In infant schools, a number of situations can arise where sex discrimination is an obvious problem and the points listed below might help teachers to ensure that sex discrimination does not take place or at least is minimised.

1. Boys are not stronger than girls, yet teachers invariably give the boys the jobs requiring strength. Avoid asking only the boys to get out equipment. Girls are just as capable.

2. Younger boys do like rough-and-tumble but many of them can also enjoy moving to music and can display very sensitive and delicate movements if allowed. Girls can enjoy strong and dynamic movements. Avoid splitting the class into groups with such instructions as 'Boys you can be soldiers and move to this marching music! Girls you can be ballet dancers and move to this light, tinkling music!'

3. Avoid planning lessons that cater for the seemingly endless energy that boys display. The girls will always fit in of course, but this is discrimination.

4. Try not to use gender-related or sexist language such as 'Take a large ball each, you boys use it for football practice.' 'Girls take the small balls, boys take the large balls', etc.

5. Avoid dividing the class into groups according to sex by asking the children to 'Make two lines by the door', rather than 'One line of boys and one line of girls.'

6. Avoid using male or female similes such as 'Fly like superman', and say 'You can choose, move like superman or superwoman.'

Discriminating on the grounds of race is a more difficult problem.

On the whole, infant and pre-school staff do not discriminate in PE activities. The children and their parents are more likely to present problems. For instance, some parents want to retain their own culture even though they have chosen to live in Britain. Some schools, particularly in areas where there is a high percentage of children from non-British cultures, have made honest and real attempts to accommodate parents' wishes. The school staff have become familiar with the games that are traditional within the cultural life of those children and have played them with the children. Children who are required to dress in particular ways because of their culture have also been accommodated wherever possible.

REFERENCES

1. Mathews and Mathews, *The Early Mathematics Experience Kit* (Schools Council, 1987).

2. J. Bennett and R. Smith, *Bright Ideas for Science* (Ward Lock, 1984).

3. L.D. Zaichkowsky, L.B. Zaichkowsky & T.J. Martinek, *Growth and Development* (Mosby, 1980).

4. P. Clift, S. Cleave & M. Griffin, *The Aims, Role and Development of Staff in the Nursery* (NFER, 1979).

5. H. Spencer, *The Principles of Psychology* (New York, 1873).

6. F. Froebel, *Pedagogies in Kindergarten* (London, 1895).

7. P. Wetton, 'Some observations of interest in locomotor and gross motor activities in the nursery school', *P.E. Review*, vol. 6, no. 2 (1983), pp. 124–9.

8. C. Hutt, *Males and Females* (Penguin, London, 1972).

9. S. Isaacs, *The Nursery Years* (Routledge & Kegan Paul, London, 1938).

10. Spencer, *The Principles of Psychology*.

11. C. Hutt, *Males and Females* (Penguin, London, 1972).

12. S. Miller, *The Psychology of Play* (Penguin, London, 1971).

13. P. Wetton, 'Some observations of interest in locomotor and gross motor activities in the nursery school'.

14. J.M. Tanner, *Education and Physical Growth*, 2nd edn (Hodder and Stoughton, London, 1978).

15. L.M. Stallings, *Motor Learning from Theory to Practice* (Mosby, 1982).

16. PEA, Ling House, 160 Kings Cross Road, London WC1X 9DH.

17. DES, 'The Curriculum from 5 to 16', in *Curriculum Matters 2* (HMSO, 1985).

18. M. Bate, M. Smith, J. James, *Review of Tests and Assessments in Early Education (3–5 years)* (NFER, 1982).

19. M. Bate & M. Smith, *Manual for Assessment in Nursery Education* (NFER, 1978).

20. DES, *Education Observed 3: Good teachers* (HMSO, 1980).

3

Health-Related Fitness

Health education and health-related fitness have always been fundamental concepts in physical education. In this day and age, however, they seem to have become even more vital to our way of life. Public concern about all aspects of health makes it imperative that teaching programmes in schools should reflect a commitment to sound health education for all children.

It is encouraging that at the time of writing there are a number of projects which illustrate this general concern for health and fitness in schools. Some of these are worthy of mention at the outset of this chapter. The Health Education Council, for example, have produced a project called 'My Body'[1] which is, as its name suggests, a project structured to make children aware of their bodies and how their bodies work. On the whole, the material seems to be more suitable for junior school children than for infant school children, but teachers will find the notes provided very valuable for oral work with younger children.

Scholastic Publications[2] have produced a poster pack with accompanying notes which will help younger children to understand the shape and size of different internal and external parts of their bodies and how their muscles work. The notion that 'exercise keeps you fit' is also explored.

A new project which is being sponsored by the Health Education Council in conjunction with the Physical Education Association is now in preparation.[3-4] The project is to be aimed at primary school children and is titled 'The Happy Heart Project'. According to the literature, 'one of the main aims of this project is to develop approaches to educating primary age pupils about physical activity and health'. The main thrust of the programmes is to encourage teachers to include health-related fitness awareness activities in their lessons so that children become knowledgeable about the need to develop active lifestyles if they are to remain healthy.

A publication which spans the whole of the statutory school age range is 'Health Education from 5–16'.[5] This is a discussion document, which is part of the 'Curriculum Matters', an HMI series. The document outlines 16 objectives which could be reached at the end of the primary phase. The importance of exercise, exercise in the outdoors, the health hazard of obesity and the importance of understanding the names and functions of parts of the human body are all stated objectives for the health education curriculum, which are included in the discussion document. Clearly, then, health education and fitness is a priority for all teachers for all children at all stages of development.

It goes without saying that early childhood educators should also respond to the new awareness about health-related fitness and the need for children to develop active lifestyles, since research[6] now shows that the earliest changes leading to heart disease begin early in life. Case studies are showing that even six-year-old children, when examined, are displaying high blood pressure, high cholesterol levels and some evidence of coronary heart disease. Research is also indicating that any change in a child's lifestyle must be made early in life if that child is to grow into a fit and healthy adult. Another reason why health awareness in early childhood is important, is that dietary and exercise habits are easier to change during the primary school years but become increasingly difficult with the onset of puberty. It would seem then, that children cannot be encouraged to start exercising too early in life.

All fitness programmes, however, should be planned carefully, keeping in mind the age and capacities of the children. Adult programmes should not be adapted and used with young children, rather, the programmes should be planned so that children are exposed to varied activity which has an emphasis on stimulating the cardio-respiratory system and on providing enough vigorous large motor activity to increase strength and encourage growth. Teachers should remember, too, the importance of 'feeling good', since children who are physically healthy are more able to function properly in intellectual and social interchange.

Many early childhood educators have been sceptical about providing teacher-directed PE sessions in pre-school institutions, let alone thinking of looking specifically at exercises which will assist children to become physically fit. The good work of the McMillan[7] era has slipped away and we no longer seem to believe in the universal value of physical exercise in the outdoors. Lip service is only paid to providing large motor experiences for our younger children. If we could be confident that all pre-schools provided stimulating and challenging environments, that every child took part in vigorous exercise, that boys and girls had equal opportunities for physical play and that three- and four-year-olds experienced progressive physical experience, then there would be no need to press for more teacher-directed activities for universal health and fitness.

However, two observational studies (Cooper, 1977; Wetton, 1978) have shown quite clearly that this is not the case. Both studies observed children in pre-school settings during their free-choice play sessions. Cooper[8] was able to demonstrate the importance of the presence and interaction of the teacher in the area of large motor activities, if children were to be involved in movement activities. Wetton[9] found that the inequality of provision in some pre-school establishments affected the kind and quality of locomotor and gross motor play with which the children became involved. Both studies, together with many others (Hutt, Packer, *et al.*) also showed the irrefutable evidence that boys are more interested in choosing to play on large apparatus than girls and that boys are much more interested in chasing and vigorous activity than are girls. The studies also showed that there were instances which showed that girls moved away from an activity if boys began to play vigorously. It seems likely, then, that girls can be affected by the boys' behaviour in choosing activities. Another observable factor in Wetton's studies[9] was that four-year-olds were no longer interested in choosing certain physical activities which were thought to be important and yet, the three-year-olds were. A possible interpretation of these observations might be that the four-year-olds were no longer being challenged. It could also be argued that the teachers were relying on open-ended experience as a foundation for physical fitness and physical development and in doing this they were denying their own role as teachers and directors of activities. In this context, it is perhaps relevant to consider what Piaget[10] has said about this:

> While the young child is impelled by its own inner tendencies to undertake a continual organising process of its experiences and so retain the results for use in subsequent attempts, some form of systemisation by the adult would not be wholly harmful.

Early childhood teachers should, therefore, consider a structured programme of fitness activities that will ensure that all the children are physically conditioned to resist all the stresses of their environment without undue fatigue and still have enough energy left to play with their friends. A possible way of doing this is as follows:

SUGGESTED GUIDELINES

1. Provide a generous amount of locomotor and gross motor activity at least three times each week.
2. Incorporate as many fitness activities as possible into the play environment.
3. Plan teacher-child activities which will develop specific physical qualities — strength, stamina and flexibility.

Strength

Strength is the ability of a muscle or groups of muscles to exert force. The improvement in strength is necessary for the development of physical fitness, (remember that the heart is a muscular organ!) and that muscles need to be made to work progressively harder if they are to become stronger. Muscular strength is important for life skills, sports skills and for maintaining good posture. Strength can be gained when the muscles of the body are put under stress as they tense and relax repeatedly during vigorous activity.

Stamina

Stamina is a term used to describe a person's ability to carry on using muscular effort over a period of time. In order to develop stamina, the child needs both muscular strength and a progressive ability to carry out vigorous activities without undue breathing stress.

Flexibility

Flexibility is a term used to describe the range of movements possible at the joints. Children need movement activities which will encourage them to force their joints into the maximum ranges of movement.

SUGGESTED ACTIVITIES

First of all, analyse your existing programme. In pre-schools, have a look at your environment with your 'fitness spectacles' on. Be critical and observant. Are all the children active or just a few? Should you build in more teacher-directed activities? Consider your programme of teacher-directed activities and assess its value for fitness development potential. In the infant school, evaluate your programme critically. Does the programme enable the children to develop the three necessary ingredients for physical fitness?

In free-play situations, can the children be guided and stimulated to extend their own movements? Next, consider the daily programme and attempt to include some activities requiring both strength and flexibility and some exercises to stimulate the cardio-vascular system to build up stamina and endurance. Cardio-vascular activities are listed first, since these are often good ways of starting a lesson.

Cardio-vascular activities:

Rhythmic movement

Action songs, moving to a drum beat and jumping on the spot are suitable activities. For example for '*Here we go round the Mulberry Bush*', make a large circle and walk clockwise, holding hands.

Here we go round the Mulberry Bush
                the Mulberry Bush
                the Mulberry Bush
Here we go round the Mulberry Bush
On a cold and frosty morning.

This is the way we wash our hands
              wash our hands
              wash our hands
This is the way we wash our hands
On a cold and frosty morning.

Again joining hands, repeat the first verse, this time skipping. The second verse can be repeated replacing 'wash our hands' by 'hop on the spot', then 'jump on the spot', 'turn around' and finally, 'jog on the spot', etc.

Or with '*The Grand Old Duke of York*', march smartly on the spot lifting the knees and swinging arms whilst singing the first line. Then, 'He had 10,000 men' — stretch out ten fingers (still marking on the spot). 'He marched them up to the top of the hill' — stretch the arms high (still marking on the spot). 'And he marched them down again', — crouch down small. 'And when they were up they were up' — stretch the arms high (still marching on the spot). 'And when they were down they were down' — crouch down small. 'And when they were only half-way up' — stretching arms straight out in front (still marching). 'They were neither up nor down' — stretch arms first high then crouch down (still marching).

Running

1. Running anywhere steadily.
2. Running quickly for a short distance and stopping suddenly.
3. Running quickly, stopping and jumping on the spot.
4. Curling up small or hopping on one leg.
5. Running over a ten metre distance.
6. Chasing games.
7. Follow-my-leader.

Jumping

1. On the spot with feet together.
2. Over a distance with feet together like a kangaroo.
3. Skipping with a rope or hoop.

Hopping

1. On the spot, then on the left foot, then the right foot.
2. Hopping anywhere on the left foot, then the right foot.
3. Hopping on the left foot for ten metres and back to start with the right foot.

Dramatic ideas

1. Galloping like a horse.
2. Flying like an aeroplane (running with arms outstretched).
3. Flying like batman/batwoman.
4. Swooping like a bird.

Dancing to recorded music or percussion

1. Stretching high, low, and wide.
2. Running to the beat of a drum.
3. Shaking the body, arms, legs, trunk, head.
4. Shaking as the body stretches high then low.
5. Jerky movements — a robotic style, using each movable part of the body.
6. Floppy movements like a rag doll — on the spot and moving in the room.
7. Skipping to the beat of a drum.
8. Shaking to the rattle of a tambourine.
9. Robotic movements to the click of the castanets.

With partners

1. One curls up on the floor the other jumps over him. Half the group jump over all the curled-up bodies and then change places.
2. One child makes a bridge, the other climbs under and then jumps over.
3. The children carry a hoop between them and on a signal, they put it on the ground and jump in and out of the hoop.

Any of these selected activities must be repeated steadily until the teacher observes that the children are beginning to 'puff'. Eventually it will be possible to build up the length of time before the 'puffing' begins. One, two, or even three activities might eventually be included in each lesson.

Strength activities

It is important to provide activities which will help to develop the three main areas of the body: the legs, the trunk and the arm-shoulder areas. Some activities will involve the use of all three areas at once, but teachers should try to balance the sessions so that each part of the body is used. Teachers will need to be vigilant observers if muscular strength is to be developed since children have to be involved sufficiently in exercise so that they are challenged to make a greater effort. The teacher must also ensure that the children perform the activities properly. For example:

1. 'Roger taps with one hammer, one hammer, one hammer.'
   (Clench the left fist, hammer with the left arm.)
   'Roger taps with two hammers, two hammers, two hammers.'
   (Clench the right fist and hammer with both arms.)
   'Roger taps with three hammers, three hammers, three hammers'.
   (Stamp on a left foot and hammer with both arms.)
   'Roger taps with four hammers, four hammers, four hammers.'
   (Stamp on left and right feet alternately and hammer with both arms.)
2. Sit with the legs stretched out, encourage the children to tense the muscles and stretch the toes.
3. Sit and bend the knees with the feet tucked near the seat. Stretch the legs out and then curl them.
4. Jack-in-the-box. Curl up small. Jump up, stretch the whole body and return to a curled position.
5. Jump over a hoop which is flat on the floor.
6. Jump into and out of the hoop with both feet together.
7. Jump around the outside of the hoop with both feet together.
8. Hop around the outside of the hoop first with the left foot and then the right foot.
9. Jump on and off a gymnastic bench with the feet only.
10. Jump over the gymnastic bench from side to side.
11. Jump over the gymnastic bench.
12. Race across 10 metres — running, hopping, etc.
13. Run up sloping banks.
14. Walk up sloping planks.
15. Run around objects, e.g. six small mats placed in a line equidistant from each other.
16. Jump over the six mats, one after the other.
17. Tap feet to music — the right foot, the left foot, alternate feet.
18. Balance on one foot for as long as possible.
19. Assume a sitting position, take the weight on the feet and legs — hold the position.
20. Hop around two markers, five metres apart. (Or around a partner, five metres away.)

Exercises to develop the trunk

1. Reach high with the right arm.
2. Reach high with the left arm.
3. Cross the arms across the chest, then stretch them wide.
4. Stretch high with both arms.
5. Bend gently at the waist and let the fingertips touch the toes.
6. Make a banana shape whilst lying down.
7. Make a lop-sided shape.
8. 'Can you make more bendy shapes?'
9. Curl the top part of the body in to the waist, make the body 'tight'.
10. Lie down and lift the legs in the air. 'Cycle' with the legs.
11. Sit on the floor with the legs straight out and touch the toes.
12. Lie down. Bend in the middle, lift the legs towards the head — try to touch the floor beyond the head with the toes.
13. Stand with feet apart, twist the body at the waist and look over the left, then the right, shoulder.
14. Sit with the legs stretched out, twist and put the hands on the floor behind the back.
15. Stretch the arms behind the body until the palms touch.
16. Bend the left arm over the left shoulder, bend the right arm behind the back; try to let the right fingers touch the left fingers.

Exercises to develop the arms and shoulder girdle

1. Circle the right arm forwards, then backwards, right, then left then both together, like swimming the back crawl.
2. Make a circle with the right shoulder, keeping the arm at the side of the body, then the left shoulder, then both together.
3. Shrug the shoulders up and down, right then left, then both together.
4. Make a circle with the shoulders — the right, the left, then both together.
5. Practise the breast stroke action, then the front crawl action.
6. Sit down and practise rowing a boat.
7. Sit down and practise paddling a canoe.
8. Put the hands on the head with elbows pointing outwards. Bring the elbows towards each other. Try to make them touch.
9. Keep the hands on the head, lift first the right and then the left elbow as high as possible.

10. Pretend to climb a ladder. Reach high with alternate hands.
11. Stretch the arms wide, palms facing the sky. Slowly reach up and clap the palms above the head. Turn the palms outwards and clap the hands behind the back.
12. Put the body weight on two hands, use the toes to balance the body. Count to five.
13. Crawl along like a caterpillar. Start in a crouched position, move the hands in front of the body as far as possible then walk the feet to meet the hands.
14. With the weight on two hands, lift one leg high then the other.
15. With the weight on two hands, kick both legs in the air. (Like a kicking donkey.)

Flexibility

Many of the activities listed under the heading of strength exercises are also flexibility exercises. Generally speaking, the children need activities that allow them to bend all their joints, to twist and rotate their joints and to stretch the whole body and parts of the body. Examples include:

1. 'Can you stretch further?'
2. 'Try and stretch your legs and toes as you hang.'
3. 'Tense your muscles, tight, tight, as you clench your fists.'
4. 'Twist your body further.'
5. 'Reach out — more, more —.'

Pre-school educators can serve their children best by providing three short sessions of health-related exercise each week. It would be advisable to separate the children into age groups for this activity because once a programme has been established, the older children will be much fitter than the younger ones. A good way to proceed is to select some activities from each of the suggested lists and to alternate them. Obviously children cannot cope with the physical stress of too many cardio-vascular activities or too many arm-strengthening activities all in one session! Choose activities from the beginning of the lists first and eventually select further activities as the children get older and become more physically conditioned.

Infant teachers may want to integrate the health-related exercises into a normal lesson. In this case, the teacher should look at her plan for each lesson and check the lists to ensure that each of her lessons

contains some of the exercises that will promote growth and development in the ways indicated. Try to make the children aware of the
purpose of the fitness activities even at the three-year-old level. Talk
to them about what you are doing together — 'We are going to make
our arms stronger now,' or 'We are going to practise our running
so that we don't get tired when we run to catch the bus,' or 'I thought
we might do some bending and stretching today to make our chests
and tummies strong,' or 'Shall we try and make our hearts happy
today?' As children get older, they can be given more information,
particularly when they are using 'My Body' or 'Ourselves' as themes
in the classroom. Top infants can be encouraged to use a stopwatch
to time short-distance runs and record their times. They could also
be challenged to see how far they can run in four seconds. Each child
can be given a bean bag which is placed on the ground after the first
run. After the first attempt, they can be challenged to see if they can
run beyond the bean bag in four seconds. The teacher can act as both
starter and timekeeper.

Children should always be kept informed about the reasons for
exercising and given as much information as possible, as and when
they become conceptually able to absorb it. Remember to make the
activities enjoyable. Try not to set targets or goals which are too difficult to achieve. Our main purpose in this kind of work should be
to try to encourage children to enjoy active play so that they develop
a positive attitude to physical activity and therefore continue to be
active all their lives. We must, in all physical education lessons,
encourage children to develop lifestyles that include regular physical
activity if they are to remain healthy.

REFERENCES

1. HEC, *My Body* (Heinemann Educational Books, 1984).
2. Scholastic Publications, *My Body Poster Pointers* (1985).
3. HEC, *Newsletter for the Health and Physical Education Project* (Loughborough University, 1986).
4. HEC, *Newsletter of the Health and Physical Education Project* (Hull University, 1986).
5. DES, 'Health Education from 5–16', *Curriculum Matters 6* (HMSO, 1986).
6. J.G. Albinson & G.M. Andrews, *The Child in Sport and Physical Activity* (University Park Press, 1976).
7. M. McMillan, *The Nursery School* (Dent, London, 1919).
8. M. Cooper, *Observational Studies in Nursery School* (Durham, 1977).
9. P. Wetton, 'Some observations of interest in locomotor and gross motor

4

The Importance of Physical Play and Curriculum Content in Pre-schools

THE IMPORTANCE OF PHYSICAL PLAY

Many pre-schools appear to have dispensed with the philosophy that was promoted by the McMillan sisters in the early part of the century, which focused attention on the basic health of the child as a foundation for the child's total development. The sisters believed in the importance of exercise in the fresh air, a balanced diet and adequate sleep.

Since the McMillan[1] era, there has been a steady movement towards an emphasis on developing the child's intellect and cognition through fine motor play rather than allowing children to experience the gross motor and locomotor play which is so important to their all-round development in the early years. Susan Isaacs[2] went as far as to state that free play and access to the outdoors was important in helping children restore their 'psychic equilibrium'.

Most pre-school personnel would agree that the physical development and physical growth of young children is important, but it is very easy to take this entirely for granted. Indeed it could be argued that, in recent years, this is precisely what has happened. Inevitably, and barring accidents, children grow, their muscles become stronger and they move with dexterity. They do so without apparent outside help. However, it is not until we notice a four-year-old child in a two-year-old body or a child who is clumsy that we begin to look specifically at how children grow, develop and become more co-ordinated and begin to think how we can help them become more physically proficient.

Most early childhood educators would suggest that movement is central to the play and learning of pre-school children, just as most physical educationists would suggest that children learn to move when they are involved in physical education activities. The word 'movement' however, is a general and all-embracing word which does not entirely explain the specificity of the tasks in practical terms. It is therefore important to re-state the importance of physical play in the life of the young child so that teachers are clear about what is meant by 'moving to learn' and movement being 'central' to the learning of young children. It is important to re-state the importance of physical play for the following reasons:

1. Exercise, preferably outdoors, is an essential requirement for healthy growth and development.
2. Motor skill learning is important for survival.
3. Motor activity is essential for the strengthening of muscles and bones and for increasing manual dexterity.
4. There is a relationship between motor experience and cognitive development.[3-4]
5. Gross limb — eye co-ordination and fine motor — visual co-ordination rely on physical practice.
6. Physical activity helps to develop conceptualisation.
7. Self-concept can be built and established, with the help of the teacher, through successful physical play.
8. The social, emotional and moral development of children can be advanced through physical activity with the help and intervention of the teacher.
9. It is becoming evident that exercise patterns should be developed early in life to prevent heart disease and obesity in later years.

Pre-school teachers who understand the importance of physical play will realise the value of planning a good physical environment when attempting to nurture a child's growth and development, since in the early years, the child spends most of his day in constantly exploring his environment. Activity is essential to him since he shows little inclination or desire to sit down for any length of time. He seeks for challenges and wanders around from one activity to another, staying for varying amounts of time, constantly busy, though having a short attention span. He is variously involved in activities which give him practice in controlling his body and using parts of his body in different ways so that he learns new concepts and advances his physical skills. He is undoubtedly learning through movement play. It is therefore crucially important for pre-school leaders to consider which types of play will help him to extend his learning.

FREE PLAY AND STRUCTURED PLAY

Children's play (within a pre-school establishment) has often been categorised into two main forms — free play and structured play.

Free play is play selected by the child within the constraints of his environment. The child is allowed to move about the areas, freely choosing his own physical play. This gives him an excellent medium for practising and developing his motor skills at his own pace and within his own capabilities. On the other hand, structured play is play that is teacher-directed. The teacher structures a particular situation and sets out to involve the child in a particular learning process. Structured play is goal-orientated and can be planned either for an individual child or for a group of children. The planning of the physical environment then is *crucial* if provision is to be made for these two forms of play.

PLANNING ENVIRONMENTS FOR PHYSICAL PLAY INDOORS

In England, the provision for physical play is varied and often not provided with the child's home environment in mind. This is a disappointment to committed pre-school teachers. There is also a variation in provision between nursery schools, nursery classes and pre-school play groups and it is often the nursery class which has least provision, particularly in relation to gross physical play and locomotor play. Many observational studies [5-7] have highlighted the need for children to be free to climb, to slide, to run, to chase and also to be generally involved in 'rough-and-tumble' activity.

In any pre-school establishment, then, there should be six fundamental requirements for physical play indoors:

1. The provision of a multi-purpose climbing frame.
2. The provision of toys with wheels.
3. The provision of large building blocks.
4. The freedom to walk about the establishment without restriction.
5. A space and a suitable surface for children to be involved in 'rough-and-tumble'.
6. A space for teacher-directed activity.

Where space is really limited, particularly in nursery classrooms, children should have access to the infant school hall to have the opportunity to use climbing apparatus and toys with wheels and for 'rough-and-tumble' activities and teacher-directed play. Ideally, the hall should be made available for all free-choice periods in the nursery, but where this is not possible, then the nursery children should have a recognised period allocated in the timetable each day. If basic indoor provision of this kind is not available, then it is essential for children to have free access to outdoor play of a similar nature in all free-choice periods. If this is still not possible, then it follows that proper provision is being denied the children.

Nurseries that have an indoor area specially designated for gross motor and locomotor activities can build up their provision from the six fundamental requirements mentioned previously and also plan to provide some, or all, of the following apparatus to complement this provision:

1. A see-saw;
2. Hobby horses;
3. Barrels;
4. A roundabout;
5. Ladders;
6. A rocking boat;
7. Tricycles;
8. A tumbling mat;
9. Cardboard boxes (packaging material);
10. Steps (or blocks to make into steps);
11. Balance boards.

Many commercial companies make custom-built equipment so the selection of suitable apparatus must be considered very carefully. The following list suggests the points to take into consideration when selecting equipment:

1. The equipment should be safe. Edges and joints should be rounded and any protrusions should have a rubber stopper in a different colour to indicate a possible danger area. There should be no moving parts that might trap small fingers. Apparatus that has been made specifically for young children should be selected — not too tall, nor the spaces too wide, etc.

2. The equipment should have many uses. Teachers and children should be able to vary the layout of their P.E. equipment. A

'best buy' is a climbing frame with detachable and attachable parts that can be lifted and manoeuvred by the children.

3. The equipment should provide different challenges. Choose pieces of apparatus that provide the children with different kinds of challenges. Basic differences, for example, a slide as opposed to a ladder and also apparatus which is exciting like a 'merry-go-round' or a 'pogo-stick' should be considered.

4. The equipment should provide colour wherever possible.

5. The equipment should be a mixture of wood, metal, plastic, etc., to provide the children with different tactile experiences.

The positioning of the pieces of equipment needs careful thought and the surface on which they are going to be placed must be considered. The floors of many pre-school areas for large pieces of apparatus have fitted carpets and these are thought to be satisfactory since the children seem to find the softer surface more welcoming. (The carpet also helps to deaden some of the noise!) It also prevents hazards such as the movement of static equipment, which could occur on a wooden floor. The arrangement of the apparatus must be planned with safety in mind. Clearly, if children are to be allowed to play freely on the large pieces of apparatus, then the adults must be confident that the apparatus is stable and that any rotating pieces are surrounded by a clear space. Open spaces should be left to accommodate vigorous bursts of activity. One teacher should be designated to be responsible for such an area or at least have it in clear view.

PLANNING ENVIRONMENTS FOR PHYSICAL PLAY OUTDOORS

The outdoor area should be a continuation of the indoor environment and the doors to the outside area should always be open. Children like to be outside and usually choose to play outdoors for varying amounts of time in the free-choice periods. It is the author's view that it is more natural to allow free access than to have a 'timetabled' half hour. Many hours of observation would seem to confirm this view. Research has also shown[8] that working-class children seem to learn more when playing outside. It is therefore, perhaps, important for teachers to consider very carefully which system is best for their children. The modern notion is that wherever possible, the outdoor area should be part of the natural environment. School architects are much more enlightened nowadays and if teachers can be invited to work with them at the planning stage, then the environment can be both exciting and educational.

In an ideal outdoor environment there should be grassed areas and paved areas, both of which are flat. There should also be a grassy bank of some kind. When a new environment is being planned, it is possible to use the soil, which has been excavated to level a surface, to make banks or mounds that will provide children with uneven and sloping surfaces for running and rolling down. Trees and bushes should be planted to give children an awareness of the 'outdoors'. The teacher should consider the types of trees and bushes that will best enhance both the children's play and their learning. For example, some evergreen and some deciduous trees and bushes should be planted. Plant different, but hardy, flowering herbage. Trees can eventually be used for tree houses or for limited rope swinging. Bushes can be used as places to run round or hide behind, etc. Any fallen logs or streams should also be used to advance physical play and there should be an area of soil set aside for digging.

The choice of equipment to place in such an environment must be selected with the following principles in mind:

1. Safety;
2. Advancing physical skills and physical development;
3. Imaginative and creative play;
4. Excitement and challenge.

1. Equipment should be vandal-proof. Metal tubular frames are the least susceptible to damage. Sand pits must be fitted with a lockable lid to prevent deposits of broken glass or dog excrement. Where this proves impossible, then the pit must become a sand tray on a trolley that can be stored indoors. All non-fixed apparatus should be stored in a lock-up shed.
2. A variety of equipment should be provided which has been selected with children's development in mind. If there are both indoor and outdoor environments available, then the one should complement the other. If only an outdoor environment is provided, then teachers should begin by making provision for the six basic requirements listed previously on page 47 for indoors.
3. Much of the equipment which is provided for the advancement of physical skills and development will allow children to develop their play from pure physical play into allied creative and imaginative play.
4. The area should look so challenging and exciting that it is

difficult to resist!

Some of the following ideas can help teachers with this aspect.

SUGGESTED EQUIPMENT

A variety of equipment should be chosen based on the six basic requirements indicated for the indoor environment:

A climbing frame — tree house.
A slide.
Steps.
A plank to balance on — about 50 cm high, or a bridge.
Space to move at speed.
Blocks or tree stumps driven into the ground.
Rubber car tyres both secured and unattached.
A disused boat?
A caravan?
A garden house.
A see-saw.
A rocking boat.
Planks, ladders, boxes, small barrels, blocks, etc.
Large balls, bats, bean bags, hoops, quoits.
Ropes.
Targets — cones, cans, etc.
Tricycles — scooters — go carts.
Prams — Trucks.
Buckets, spades, sieves, watering cans, etc., (sand play).
A ball on a tether and stand.
Ropes and rope ladders.
Used cable spools.
A large tug-of-war type rope.
Large toy cars, lorries and vans to load and push.
Obstacles to jump over and off.
Stepping stones.
Circles and squares painted on the ground.

Unfortunately, teachers are seldom invited to the planning stage of either indoor or outdoor environments and are seldom consulted about the construction of outdoor environments. The usual scenario is one of teachers trying to adjust to the constraints of an area which has been provided for them. The ideal situation does exist in some locations, but where it does not, teachers should revert to the suggested six basic requirements and petition the authorities until the essentials are provided.

THE MATERIAL

The material to be provided for children in this age group should be selected with two main forms of play in mind — 1. Child-selected play; 2. Teacher-directed play.

1. CHILD-SELECTED PLAY

If the child is allowed to select his play in an educational establishment, then the teacher must be aware of what he is learning from his environment. It is important therefore, for teachers to analyse the physical environment and to have a sound knowledge of its learning potential. For instance, an analysis of activity on the climbing frame gives an indication of its value to children as a physical play experience.

The climbing frame

Upper and lower body development, balance control, co-ordination, visual perception, body awareness, laterality and tactile perception are developed.

Different methods of access

These include 1. a narrow ladder frame; 2. a window frame; 3. a sloping ladder; 4. a sloping plank.

1. The narrow ladder (rungs with small spaces between) can be used initially to give gentle access for new children. Finger, hand, arm, trunk, leg, and foot muscles are used in this activity. The child will usually reach out with both hands to start his climb, but laterality will be encouraged as he ascends. The usual pattern is right hand, left hand, hold with both hands, right foot, left foot. It will be some time before the child displays true laterality and the right hand/arm and left leg/foot move together on the ascent.

2. The window frame is a more challenging point of access in that greater use of the muscles is needed to reach across the space between the rungs.

3. The sloping ladder is a natural progression from the two methods of access already described. The movement still demands the use of the hands and feet, but is more challenging since the child must negotiate a slope. This method of access depends to some extent on tactile discrimination and visual perception as the child searches for his next foothold and his next handhold.

4. The sloping plank is a challenge of a different kind, since its use demands balance and more lower-leg strength, together with tactile discrimination and visual perception.

Activities on the climbing frame

1. Up and down;
2. Under and through;
3. Over;
4. Balancing;
5. Hanging;

Up and down. At first, children will select how high they want to climb and know their own limits. In the early stages, children may only climb up two rungs and climb down again. Some may climb onto one rung only, hold on for some time and come down again. This activity is an extension of climbing stairs.

The next stage is often to climb up to a platform and sit. (Platforms are useful motivators for timid climbers!)

The next stage is often to climb up to a point where there is the opportunity to slide down. (Another motivator.)

Confidence in climbing should increase after practice and any child who is observed to be finding difficulty after one term should be given help.

Under and through. Children who select to go under the bars etc. and through the spaces are beginning to display large-motor confidence and the first signs of creativity. Children often begin to explore in this way quite by chance. Sometimes the activity is the product of 'nosiness,' one child poking his head through to watch another child in action, or it is the product of an exchange of conversation where one child has to 'lean through' or 'look under' to talk to another child. Going under and through frames gives children practice in bending and manoeuvring the trunk in ways that are not possible in vertical climbing. Again, it enhances tactile and visual discrimination and begins to stimulate more use of finger, hand and wrist muscles.

Over. When children begin to climb over parts of the climbing frame, teachers should be able to observe a noticeable progression in development. The child is displaying his new-found tactile ability, his balance control, his motor strength (both fine and gross) and his creative ability. Initially, this activity occurs at lower levels, but when the child can show dexterity in climbing over the top rung of the climbing frame, he is ready for new challenges which self-selection may not provide. Such a child may move to a lower level and experiment with going over a lower rung with a somersault, but again, this is unlikely to occur from self-selection unless he has observed another child doing it.

Balancing. Learning balance control demands practice. Everyone is aware of how much practice is needed to acquire an upright stable stance and a similar amount of practice is required to control both static and dynamic balance on different surfaces. It must be remembered that to make any kind of movement with stability, a child must be able to balance himself. Many teacher-guided activities will be necessary for most children to accomplish this. The climbing frame can provide both a motivator and a practice station. A sloping plank gives the child the chance to practise walking up and down and to practise holding a stationary position at some point on the slope. A balance beam, not less than the width of a gymnastic form and suspended at a low level so that children can step off, is an excellent practice activity for both static and dynamic balance.

Hanging. The low rungs of a window frame provide the opportunity for children to begin to be involved in hanging activities. (Although later on, they can be observed hanging and dropping from heights of 6 feet.) The child will probably start by standing and leaning against the frame and will bend over the rung as he talks to another child. This first bending will increase spine mobility. Some children will hang on with hands, arms and trunks and let the feet swing free, which will be the first stage in developing the necessary strength in the arms to be able to hang from the equipment. The next stage is often achieved by mistake. A child, as he is climbing will sometimes inadvertently let go with his feet and will feel the first sensation of supporting his weight with his arms. Eventually, children will choose to hang on to a low bar with hands and knees, until, after much practice, the child will feel able to hang by his knees.

Methods of descent

These include: 1. Climbing down; 2. Crawling down; 3. Sliding; 4. Jumping; 5. Hanging and dropping.

1. Climbing down is the first method of descent and is often experienced from only a height of 10 cms. Children should be allowed to practise this as often as they need to until they feel confident and secure.

2. Crawling down is a manifestation of 'latter-day cowardice'. This is the child who has been motivated to climb up in order to slide down (having seen other children's obvious enjoyment of the activity) and who suddenly realises he does not have either the courage or often the motor knowledge to carry out the manoeuvre. The child uses his bottom, heels, and hands to come down face-side up or reverses his body and crawls down backwards. The child who crawls in these ways is actually using his muscles and exercising his joints more than the child who actually slides down in order to descend!

3. Sliding is an enjoyable, challenging and exciting activity which can be an advanced manoeuvre for the young child. He needs to balance his body, prepare for forward motion and time the release of his hand grasp. This takes courage. The sliding motion demands muscle control, particularly of the lower back, and the arrival is not necessarily pleasant in the first few practices.

4. Jumping down from the climbing frame is an advanced activity and is in fact not a jump in most instances, but a drop from a height.

5. Dropping from a secure obstacle takes courage and skill. To control the weight of the body in flight demands a particular kind of balance and the landing requires the child to bend his hips, knees and ankles. Most children will fall forward on impact and break their fall with the use of both hands. Teachers can be most helpful at this stage of development.

. The climbing frame is therefore a resource for a wide range of self-selected physical play. It is a resource or medium for exciting physical play. It is also a resource or medium for exciting creative, dramatic and fantasy play and children should be allowed to use it for this purpose when the need arises. It can become a fort, or a castle, or a Rebel Carrier, or a Battle Star Galactica! The children will still be exercising physically and advancing their motor skills and indeed may in fact extend their skill even further due to the motivating drive in dramatic situations.

Other pieces of apparatus can also be analysed for their value in helping children develop their 'movement' potential.

Toys with wheels

These toys encourage children to use their fingers and hands to manipulate handlebars and handles, their feet and legs to drive tricycles, tractors and lorries and their upper bodies and often their legs to push, pull and manoeuvre the toys. The child's kinaesthetic discrimination is enhanced as is his visual motor learning and his space awareness. There is also some advancement of his balance control and an increase in his understanding of laterality.

Large building blocks

These come in various sizes and in different materials and, in sheer physical terms, they provide the children with the capacity to learn about lifting, carrying, holding and building. As the children lift, carry and build, they are strengthening their upper bodies and both gross and fine motor control is being practised. The child's visual and tactile perception is also being advanced, as is his creative play. Teachers should analyse each piece of equipment in this way before introducing it into the nursery and be aware of its learning potential for the children.

Other child-selected play can occur at the most unusual times in the most unusual places with the most unexpected materials. One child or group of children can often build amazing structures with large building blocks and can challenge their own physical ability and create structures by self-motivation in a way that the teacher could not hope to simulate. Admittedly, these structures collapse sometimes and cause a disturbance, but to the child, even this can prove exciting and challenging.

Some teacher-provided materials do challenge children physically and provide excitement. A tree-house, or a caravan, or a large disused boat for instance can be very stimulating as can a wide sloping path along which children can cycle and run.

Rough-and-tumble

Another very popular self-selected activity is rough-and-tumble play.[9] Observational research (see Chapter 3) has indicated the necessity to provide space for this kind of play. The research has not shown why children, particularly boys, choose this form of activity, but since at the present time, early childhood educators allow most of a child's pre-school time to be centred around self-selected activity, then teachers must make provision for it and analyse the activity. Rough-and-tumble play can not be neatly categorised. It varies from vigorous and almost uncontrolled running to tumbling around on the floor. Boys tumble and roll together for no apparent reason and usually, without aggression. Children bounce about on crash mats with gurgles of delight. Many reasons can be suggested for this kind of physical play, one of which might be the often quoted 'Surplus Energy' theory (Spencer). This kind of play is very vigorous. It increases children's strength, power, endurance and flexibility and provides a large amount of large muscle activity. It is also very enjoyable for the children.

2. TEACHER-DIRECTED PLAY

The teaching material for teacher-directed play can be considered under five main headings: 1. Fitness development activities (which includes, for this purpose, basic motor skills); 2. Creative and expressive activities; 3. Rhythmic activities; 4. Games activities; 5. Specialist activities.

Fitness development activities and basic motor skills

Health-related fitness activities have already been outlined in Chapter 3. Basic motor skills consist of walking, running, hopping, jumping, skipping, bending and twisting. Teachers should select from the following activities for their five-minute or ten-minute period. The activities are listed in order of difficulty and it is suggested that teachers select the earlier activities to use with the three-year-old children.

Walking

1. Practise walking well — head up, eyes forward, tummy in, looking at a fixed point.

2. Practise walking from point A to point B in a straight line. Teaching points are to keep the toes forward, swing the arms easily, keep the back straight and adopt a normal walking stride.
3. Practise walking and stopping on the teacher's command.
4. Practise walking on the toes.
5. Long strides, short steps.
6. Walk with hands on head, etc.
7. Walk slowly, then quickly, then slowly.
8. Practise walking with the toes turned in and the toes turned out.
9. Walk heel to toe, toe to heel.
10. Walk backwards.
11. Walk with the knees high.
12. Walk on the heels.
13. Walk on the sides of the feet.
14. Walk stretching as tall as possible, then keeping as small as possible.
15. Walk forwards and on command, walk backwards.
16. Walk forwards and on command, make a full turn.

Running

1. Walk; walk quickly; run.
2. Run from point A to point B in a straight line.
3. Run as fast as you can over a specific distance. (Suggest no more than 10–15 metres.)
4. Run, touch the ground at a given place and return.
5. Run and on command, stop.
6. Traffic lights, a green bean bag for 'go', a yellow bean bag for 'slow down' and a red bean bag for 'stop'.
7. Run gently, then as fast as possible.
8. Run with little steps then big steps.
9. Run with arms stretched wide.
10. Run with stiff legs.
11. Run on the spot.

Bending

Teach the children about bending and learn together where the body can bend.

1. Explore each 'bendy bit' of the body.
2. Return to a 'bendy' jump.

3. Bend in the middle like a 'bendy' toy or a marionette whose string has been loosened.
4. Bend to make the body curled up.
5. Lie down, bend in the middle so that fingers touch the toes!
6. Practise bending forwards and backwards.
7. Practise bending from side to side.

Hopping

1. Teach the skill. Use the ball of the foot.
2. Practise on the spot with each leg.
3. Practise a hop moving forwards.
4. Hop on one leg moving forwards — see how far you can go.
5. Hop on one leg and hold the other foot.
6. Hop over a low obstacle — a skipping rope on the floor or a narrow block.

Jumping

1. Teach the skill. Bend the knees and ankles at take-off, keep the legs bent, land on the toes first.
2. Jump up and down on the spot.
3. Pretend you are bouncing on your bed. Pretend to be a bouncing ball.
4. Try little jumps, then try and jump to reach the ceiling.
5. Move forward as you jump.
6. Jump over a rope on the ground, or a bean bag, or narrow block.

Twisting

1. Keep the feet still and try and twist round the rest of your body until you can see what is behind you. Twist right then left.
2. Make your fingers twist round each other.
3. Sit down and twist your legs around each other.
4. Make your body twist — tie it into a knot!

Skipping

A number of texts on motor development suggest that a child should be able to skip at the age of four. The author has not found this necessarily to be the case, therefore, try and teach the skill. Step and hop on each foot alternately using the balls of the feet slowly and then quickly, until skipping is achieved. Speed and distance are not important but rhythm is.

LESSON PLAN — WALKING PRACTICES WITH NURSERY SCHOOL CHILDREN

Aim: To use walking practices to help children to be aware of the different ways in which they can move about the area.

Introduction

1. Follow my leader. Walk in a line behind the teacher. The teacher takes different pathways.
2. Find a space. Walk anywhere. When the teacher says stop, stand still and wave your hands in the air.
3. Run anywhere and when the teacher says stop, stand still and stretch up high.

Movement training

1. Walk towards the teacher and when she says 'stop' turn round and walk back to original place.
2. As for point 1, but when the teacher says 'stop' walk backwards back to original place.
3. Walk anywhere, on tiptoes.
4. Practise walking with long strides.
5. Practise walking with little, short steps.

Conclusion

Practise marching whilst saying the rhyme:
    The grand old Duke of York,
    He had ten thousand men,
    He marched them up to the top of the hill,
    And he marched them down again.

Creative and expressive activities

Teachers wherever possible should link these activities with the children's interests or with the theme being explored in the pre-school establishment.

Example 1: animals

After a visit to a farm, or a visit to a zoo, or after a story with pictures, practise imitating the movements of familiar creatures such as a cat, dog, bird, worm, snail, spider, horse, butterfly, rabbit, frog, etc. Use music — the piano, a guitar, a record, a tape or a percussion instrument or use descriptive words to encourage creativity and to stir the imagination — slowly, flutter, creep, canter, strut, gallop, slither, etc., or use action poems, action nursery rhymes, or games.[10] For example:

> To market to market to buy a fat pig,
> Home again, home again, jiggety jig;
> To market to market to buy a fat hog,
> Home again, home again, joggety jog.

> Incy Wincy spider climbed up the water spout,
> Down came the rain and washed the spider out,
> Out came the sunshine and dried up all the rain,
> And Incy Wincy spider climbed up the spout again.

> The farmer's dog's at my back door,
> His name is Bobby Bingo.   Skip round in a circle.
> B I N G O   Stand still and shout out
> B I N G O   the letters in turn.
>
> B I N G O   Child standing in the
> And BINGO is his name O   middle points to a child who
>   shouts B, etc, until the last child
>   who shouts 'O' who is the new
>   person in the middle.

> Mrs Brown went to town,
> Riding on a pony.
> When she came back,
> She lost her hat,
> And called on Miss Maloney.

> The scarecrow stands
> With hand in hand
> Walking is not his style
> He scares a jay,
> And a crow away
> With just a painted smile.

Three blind mice, three blind mice,
See how they run, see how they run,
They all ran after the farmer's wife,
She cut off their tails with a carving knife,
Did you ever see such a thing in your life,
As three blind mice.

Stories can help children to become creative and to express themselves. Try:

The Little Red Hen (Ladybird)

or *Chicken Licken* (Ladybird)

or *Somebody is Eating the Sun*, by Ruth Sonneburn (Random House, New York). Ruth has created a jingle for each animal, many of which have stimulating movement words.

Another story which children can be active with is *The Elephant and the Bad Baby*, by Raymond Briggs. There is a catch phrase 'Rumpeta, rumpeta, rumpeta, all down the road'. The children can be encouraged to get up and 'rumpeta'!

The elephant's walk is careful and slow,
His trunk like a pendulum swings to and fro,
But when there are children with peanuts around,
He swings it up and he swings it down.

Old MacDonald had a farm is another favourite.

Example 2: transport

After a visit to a bus station or a fire station or after a walk in the streets:

1. Move in straight lines across the room like the tractor in a field.
2. Take a quoit and drive a bus around the room.
3. Put your arms out and fly like an aeroplane.
4. Lie on your backs and cycle with your legs.
5. Move along as if you are on skates or skis.
6. Move along like a carthorse pulling a heavy cart.
7. Two children share a hoop, one child gets inside the hoop and holds it round his middle, the other child holds on to the hoop from behind. Practise being a driver and a horse.
8. Ask the children to find out how many ways they can move their bodies around the space using the feet, feet and hands, hopping, etc.

Let the children make their own sounds to accompany some of the activities, then encourage words to accompany the activities. Introduce the concept of little and big into their movements. Introduce the concept of starting and stopping. Get the children to line up one behind the other and then to move along to the following verse:

Down by the station early in the morning,
See the little puffer billies all in a row,
See the station master pull his little handle,
Puff! puff! blow! blow! off we go!

Then get them to practise walking to the train music from 'Play School'.[11]

A story that can be enjoyed together is *The Train to Timbuctoo* by M. Wise-Brown, which has a lovely catch phrase that the children can be encouraged to move to — 'Slam, Bang, grease the engine'.

If the children have been on a walk through the streets they might now enjoy:

Wee Willie Winkie runs through the town,
Upstairs and downstairs in his nightgown,
Tapping at the window, crying through the lock,
'Are the children in their beds, it's past eight o'clock.'

or make up your own two last lines to the rhyme, for example,

Driving his sports car, steering his lorry,
Reversing into a policewoman, 'Oh I'm, sorry!', etc.

Example 3: myself

This theme can be started in a PE activity period and then extended into other activities in the nursery.

1. Play music for the children to skip to, walk to, run to.
2. Practise stretching tall and wide and curling up small.
3. Practise face movements — 'We are happy', 'We are sad', 'We are angry', 'We are horrible'.
4. Make body sounds — clap hands, click fingers, plop cheeks, whistle, click tongues, snap fingers, sniff loudly, breathe loudly, etc.
5. Play different kinds of music — pop, brass band, orchestral and allow the children to move to the sound. Try and

encourage them to move in different ways. Lead with ideas and hope that they begin to feel the different moods.

6. Play music and let the children use different parts of their bodies to dance — fingers/hands/arms and toes/feet/legs.

7. Heads and shoulders knees and toes, knees and toes,
   Heads and shoulders knees and toes, knees and toes,
   Eyes and ears, and mouth and nose,
   Heads and shoulders knees and toes, knees and toes.

   Sing the whole song. The next time suggest that instead of singing 'head', they point to it instead.

8. Sing together 'Standing on one leg'.[12]

There are one or two rhymes which can be used to make them aware of the parts of their bodies:

I have ten little fingers,
And they belong to me,
I can make them do things,
Would you like to see?

I have ten little fingers,
And ten little toes,
I have a head to nod with,
And a wiggly nose.

Here is the church and here is the steeple,
Look inside and here are the people,
Here's the parson going upstairs,
And here he is a-saying his prayers.

Scrub your dirty face,
Scrub your dirty face,
With a rub-a-dub dub,
With a rub-a-dub dub,
Scrub your dirty face.

Scrub your dirty knees,

Scrub your dirty hands,

Scrub your dirty feet.[13]

Example 4: other people

The movements for this theme are more successful if explored after a visit from some of the following people: a hairdresser, musician, cook, builder, farmer, lollipop man/woman, policewoman, athlete, joiner, swimmer, etc. Take each person in turn and practise the movements that these people make. Stress the quality of the movement. For, if the example is the hairdresser, scissors move quickly — snip, snip, snip. Brushes are used gently — smooth, long, sweeping movements. The hair falls on the floor — floats, lightly down, down. The brush sweeps the hair up — strong, pushing movements, etc. This verse would be appropriate.

John is a hairdressr, snip, snip, snip,
He likes to snap his scissors, snip, snip, snip,
He brushes people's hair, down, down, down,
Snip, snip, down, down, on the ground.

Rhythmic activities

This aspect of teacher-directed physical play has an overlap with music activities and should not necessarily be separated. It is, however, helpful to children if they are allowed to express these early rhythmic motor patterns through gross motor movements and locomotor movements,

1. Walking to the beat of a drum. Marching.
2. Walk, then walk quickly as the drumbeats quicken.
3. Clapping the hands to the beat of a drum.
4. Tapping the foot to the beat of a drum.
5. Nodding the head to the beat of a drum.
6. Action songs.

Two examples of action songs are:

Here stand I
Little Jumping Joan
When nobody's with me
I'm all alone.

This is the way the ladies ride,
Tri-tree, tri-tree, tri-tree
This is the way the gentlemen ride,
Gallop-a trot, Gallop-a trot.

This is the way the farmers ride,
Hobbledy; hoy, hobbledy; hoy,
And down into the ditch!

Circle songs and games

Examples are *The farmer's in his den*, *Ring a ring a' roses* and *The grand old Duke of York*.

Other ideas

1. Join hands in a circle and walk around. When the music stops ask the children to stand still. Try and stop the music at regular intervals to create rhythm.

2. Sit down in a circle, wave the hands above the heads and when the music stops, the children must stop waving. Try to stop the music at regular intervals.

3. Bouncing on the spot with two feet together to the rhyme:

Half a pound of tuppeny rice,
Half a pound of treacle,
That's the way the money goes,
Pop goes the weasel!

4. Clapping hands to:

Pat-a-cake, pat-a-cake,
Baker's man,
Bake me a cake
As fast as you can
Pat it and prick it
And mark it with B
And put it in the oven
For baby and me.

and

We all clap hands together,
We all clap hands together,
We all clap hands together,
As children like to do!

5. For free-choice movement, play recordings of favourite nursery rhymes and songs and let the children move freely to the music.

Games activities

1. 'Jack Frost': The children run about until the teacher says 'freeze'. The children stand still and the teacher catches the wobblers!
2. 'Grandmother's Footsteps': The children and one adult creep up behind the teacher. If she hears them, she turns round. If any child moves, that child returns to the start. The child who manages to creep up on the teacher and touch her before she turns round wins.
3. 'What time is it Mr Wolf?': The children follow an adult around the room asking 'What time is it Mr Wolf?' When the adult turns round, the children 'freeze' until the adult says a time — 'Two-o'clock' and then turns around again. The game continues until the adult turns and says 'Dinner time!' At this point, the children run away and try not to be caught.
3. Chasing: Children love to move at speed and quite enjoy running across a measured distance with an adult. 'Let's see how quickly we can run across the yard!' or 'Shall we do it again?'
5. Mats or hoops: The children run anywhere and when the adult calls 'now', the children run and stand on a mat or inside a hoop.
6. Follow-my-leader: The children follow the adult and do what she does.
7. Hide-and-seek.

Skill practices

Bean bags

1. Toss the bag into the air with one hand.
2. Try for height.
3. Try for length.
4. Put four bean bags in a line two metres apart. The child runs to collect the first bag and puts it into a basket, then the second, etc.
5. Put a bean bag on the ground ten metres away from the children. Ask them to run round the bag and return to the start.
6. Place hoops around the space and ask the children to throw the bean bag inside the hoop.

7. Place five bean bags in a line one metre apart. The children run around the bean bags and straight back to the starting place.

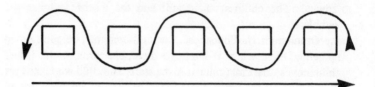

Large balls

1. Practising running and kicking a stationary ball.
2. Get the children to roll the ball away from themselves.
3. Practising tossing the ball into the air with two hands from waist height.
4. Kicking a stationary ball from a standing position.
5. Holding the ball in both hands and running around with it.
6. Rolling the ball along the ground.
7. Suspend a hoop on a rope or from a tree or a washing line. Get the children to try to toss the ball through the hoop.
8. When the paddling pool is outdoors in the summer, it is possible during a session of water play to practise throwing plastic balls into the water to see how much of a splash can be made.

Large balls should always be available for free-choice playtimes as well as for teacher-directed playtimes. Children can then practise the activities that the teacher has suggested and can also begin to explore new ways of manipulating the ball.

Specialist activities

These activities are ones selected to help a group of children or an individual within a group who seems to have a problem in relation to some aspect of their development. If a child or several children are having problems with any motor task, then the teacher needs to analyse the activity and break it down into simple stages. First of all it is important to realise that in the acquisition of any skill, it is necessary to be aware of the developmental level of the child and of the elements involved in the learning of that skill. There are likely to be perceptual, cognitive and motor elements which must be considered. The teacher's role (as has already been stated in Chapter 2), is essential in analysing the child's problem. In fact, she is the key to advancing the child's skill. (See Chapter 7.)

Where a group of children need special activities, they can be gathered together and guided by the teacher in the following way:

1. Start with a known activity so that the children enjoy success.
2. Progress in simple stages, slowly.
3. Ensure that the stages are sequential.
4. Make sure that the children understand what to do. (Make the objectives very clear).
5. Vary the tasks or present the same tasks in different ways.

For example, if the problem is an inability to balance, suggested activities could be:

1. 'The traffic light game', or walking to the music and stopping when the music stops.
2. Walking forward towards a bean bag placed three metres away, then five metres away.
3. Walking along a tape, line, or painted footsteps.
4. Standing with the eyes closed for ten seconds. The child has to try and remain completely still.
5. Walking along a low bench — the teacher holding the child's hand.
6. Walking on tiptoes.
7. Walking around an object.
8. Walking around an object on tiptoes.
9. Assisting a child to climb up and stand on a stable, wide-topped block. Asking the child to stand still whilst the teacher counts to five.
10. Walking along a low bench with the teacher walking alongside.
11. Practising walking backwards.
12. Trying to stand on one leg and then the other.
13. Trying to hop on one leg.

Some of these activities will have been practised during 'fitness activities', but for children with certain difficulties, more specific teaching is needed.

In winter, the teacher may decide that the special activities time should be used for vigorous action songs or for a further fitness session or for vigorous teacher-guided activity outdoors. Whereas in summer, the teacher might decide to bring a group indoors to play quietly on their own on the climbing apparatus with careful supervision, help and guidance.

REFERENCES

1. M. McMillan, *The Nursery Years* (Dent, 1919).
2. S. Isaacs, *The Nursery Years* (Routledge and Kegan Paul, 1938).
3. J.S. Bruner, *Studies in Cognitive Growth* (John Wiley, 1966).
4. H.G. Furth & H. Wachs, *Thinking Goes to School: Piaget's Theory into Practice*, (Oxford University Press, 1974).
5. C. Hutt, *Males and Females*, (Penguin, London, 1972).
6. M. Cooper, *Observational Studies in Nursery School*, (Durham University, 1972).
7. S. Millar, *Psychology of Play*, (Penguin, London, 1971).
8. B. Tizard, J. Philips, J. Lewis, 'Effects on Play of the Child's Social Class and of the Educational Orientation of the Centre', *J. Child Psychol. Psychiat.*, vol. 17, 1976.
9. M. Boulton & P.K. Smith, 'Rough and Tumble Play in Children, Environmental Influences, Playworld Journal', vol. 1, pp. 15–17, 1986.
10. I. Grender, *Action Songs and Rhymes* (345 Publishing Ltd., 1976).
11. Side 1, Track 4. *Sing a Song of Playschool*, BBC Recordings, REC 212
12. Side 1, Track 2. *Standing on one leg*. BBC Recordings, REC 212.
13. I. Grender, *Action Songs and Rhymes*.

5

Gymnastics in the Infant School

This chapter, and the subsequent three chapters, are concerned with the content of physical education lessons in the infant school. Suggestions are given on the planning and content of lessons for each of three age groups — the reception class, the middle infants and the top infants. Also, lesson notes are indicated where appropriate.

The term 'gymnastics' is not new in relation to the PE curriculum in infant schools. Nowadays though, the activity tends to masquerade under the title of 'large apparatus' or 'gymnastic floorwork'. However, the name we give to the subject is unimportant. It is what we teach and what the children learn that is of paramount importance. Essentially, in this aspect of PE, we are primarily concerned with the gross motor development of children. It is through this gross motor development that children learn both to manage their bodies and to exercise their large muscle groups. Eventually, having followed a careful, progressive programme of gymnastics, children should develop various physical qualities which will enable them to meet the challenges of the environment in which they live. If the programme has been efficient, then not only will the children be able to meet these challenges but they will also be able to cope with any stresses in their environment without too much fatigue and still retain enough energy to play.[1]

SAFETY POINTS

1. Make a plan if any apparatus is to be used.
2. Check the apparatus for good repair and report any defects.
3. Check the apparatus for correct assembly.
4. Check that the apparatus is accessible.

5. Beware of protrusions into the room — piano, TV, etc.
6. The children should, ideally, wear a vest and pants and work in bare feet, *never* skirts, long trousers, loose clothing, socks only, shoes or jewellery.
7. Develop a positive approach.
8. Develop a sensitive approach.
9. Make sure that non-English speaking children understand any instructions.
10. Provide an adequate 'warm-up'. This should include stretching activities followed by vigorous activity.
11. Allow the children to talk during free 'play' or exploratory parts of the lesson, but do not let the noise level rise so high that the teacher can not be heard.
12. The class must be silent when asked.
13. Teach the children how to lift, carry and manoeuvre apparatus. (Never allow apparatus to be pushed, pulled, or dragged.)
14. Divide the class into groups for apparatus work.
15. Move groups from one apparatus arrangement to another in a set order.
16. Always ask the children to move both themselves and the apparatus in a quiet, calm manner.
17. Place a mat where children are likely to land when jumping from a height.
18. Train the children to take turns and not to touch each other.
19. Train the children to walk back to wait for their next turn and to be constantly watching and looking where they are going.
20. Teachers should give help where necessary.
21. Teachers should move around the periphery of the room, keeping their backs to the walls of the room, so that the children are constantly in view.

PLANNING

The teaching of gymnastics is concerned with the teaching of skills, and if skill is to be acquired, the learning situation must be structured and progressive. In order to ensure continuity, teachers should be prepared to communicate with the teacher taking the class the following year so that the new teacher is aware of the stage the children have reached. Teachers should select lessons from the material listed and from the themes suggested. Children should reach a good standard of work (within their own capabilities) after a series of lessons before moving on to a new theme. A movement theme may last a few weeks or a few months depending on its content, the ability of the children and the number of lessons each week.

A lesson should be divided into three parts:

1. Warm-Up: A low build-up to energetic, easy movements in an effort to increase the heart rate and the rate of breathing.

2. Floorwork: A series of tasks completed without apparatus where children learn to develop skills in response to movement ideas within the theme.

3. Apparatus: Ideally children should put out the apparatus themselves. Carrying, lifting, manoeuvring and assembling are important life skills which children should learn. This also develops co-operation skills and social skills.

Lesson note — example — reception class

Aim: to make the children aware of the movements which can change the shape of the body and reinforce the 'shape' work taking place in the classroom.

Introduction:

1. Walking about the room stretching the arms and fingers high in the air to make a tall thin shape.
2. Walking about the room curled up in a small shape.
3. The teacher should use her voice to instruct the children to change from being tall to being small. Vary the speed — 'Slowly grow tall . . . small.'
4. Running anywhere and on command, making a wide shape, a small shape, a tall, thin shape.

Skill development

1. Sitting down: Practise stretching the legs and feet, stretching and curling the toes, stretching out the arms and fingers and stretching and curling the fingers — combine these after practise.
2. Still sitting down: Bend the knees, wrap the arms around the body, tuck the head in — on command 'explode' — stretch all the body parts into a wide 'star' shape.
3. Standing: Stretch tall — curl up small and assume on command, tall, small and star shapes.

Apparatus

Two benches, a movement table, four hoops and a mat are required.

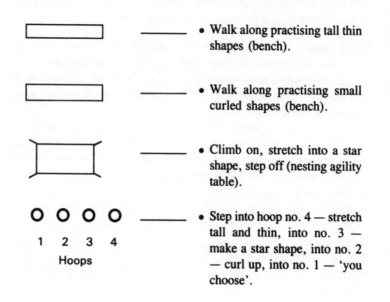

- Walk along practising tall thin shapes (bench).

- Walk along practising small curled shapes (bench).

- Climb on, stretch into a star shape, step off (nesting agility table).

- Step into hoop no. 4 — stretch tall and thin, into no. 3 — make a star shape, into no. 2 — curl up, into no. 1 — 'you choose'.

1 2 3 4

Hoops

Conclusion

1. Curl up small, jump high, be tall!
2. Walk with good posture.

APPARATUS

Children should be introduced to the use of apparatus step by step. Start by making sure that the apparatus is easily accessible. Teach the children how to collect, carry, use and return their apparatus. Go through the following stages week by week, until the children can carry the apparatus more efficiently.

Stage One

One piece of apparatus should be available for each child, preferably of the same kind, for example, one hoop each.

Stage two

Proceed to pieces of apparatus that need to be carried by more than one child. Preferably, use the same kind of apparatus, e.g. a large mat.

Stage three

Use a combination of apparatus that can be carried by a single child and apparatus that needs to be carried by two or four children. Have simple teacher-directed layouts.

Stage four

A combination of apparatus can be used, which must be checked by the teacher, for example, wall frames and larger items. If the equipment store is small, then move out the required pieces of apparatus before the lesson, with the assistance of another member of staff (or an auxiliary if there is one), before school starts or at lunchtime. (Benches can be left at the edges of the hall permanently, as they can be useful for many hall activities.)

POINTS TO REMEMBER WHEN PLANNING APPARATUS LAYOUTS

1. The planning must be based on the age, experience and ability of the children.
2. The apparatus should be chosen to correspond to the space available.
3. Teachers should make a plan with direction arrows to indicate movement and to ensure good, safe use of the space.
4. Plans should be simple at first until the children become used to lifting, carrying, positioning and the 'language of operations'.
5. Suitable apparatus should be chosen for the tasks set within the theme.
6. Try and have as many children being as active as possible at any one time within the spatial limits. Four children to an apparatus grouping is ideal. Sometimes it is necessry to have six or seven children, depending on the space available and the theme being explored.

7. Sometimes it is possible to have a layout where all the children have the same equipment (A) e.g. a mat and a bench. Sometimes more learning takes place where each group has different equipment (C) or a different arrangement of the same equipment (B).

A

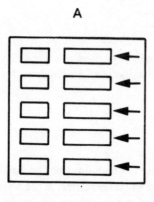

B

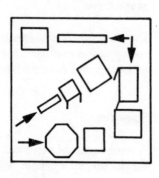

C

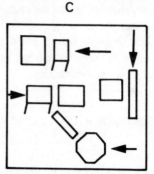

Theme: Resilience

RECEPTION CLASS CHILDREN

Reception class children should be allowed to spend time taking their clothes on and off. This is a very important life activity and the earlier these manipulative skills are learned the better. The early stages of lessons should be short. The younger the child, the shorter his attention span and his ability to cope with the demands of a large space and vigorous, yet confined activity.

However, this is the period when most rapid motor development

A suggested sequence of movement themes for gymnastic activity for infant children

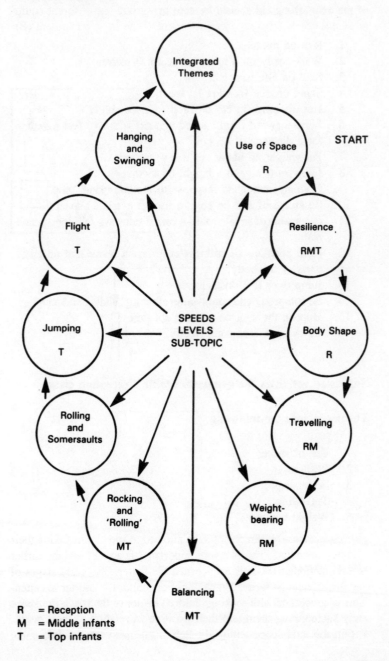

R = Reception
M = Middle infants
T = Top infants

occurs (between the ages of three and six) and most basic locomotor and fine eye-hand co-ordination skills appear and develop. At the end of the year, the child should be able to:

1.   Run on his toes.
2.   Walk easily on a narrow line for 3 metres.
3.   Skip on alternate feet.
4.   Stand on one foot for 10 seconds.
5.   Hop forward 25 cm on each foot separately.
6.   Jump forward from a standing start with two feet together for a distance of 45 cm.
7.   Put weight on hands for a few seconds.
8.   Jump vertically to a height of 8 cm.
9.   Give an immediate response to the command 'stop'.
10. Be aware of and be able to use all available space.
11. Be capable of simple rolls — curled sideways roll, long pencil roll.
12. Hold positions of stillness at different levels and on large parts of the body.
13. Jump over low obstacles.
14. Be competent and confident in climbing, sliding and hanging.
15. Hop on the spot on one leg six times.
16. Carry apparatus competently.

Suggested activities for gymnastics with a reception class

Themes include the following:

1.   Use of space;
2.   Resilience;
3.   Body shape;
4.   Travelling;
5.   Weight-bearing.

Use of space

This is concerned with making children aware of the space immediately surrounding them and their position in relation to their peers within the total space within the hall. Basic activities include:

Walking

1. Walking freely around the room (own choice).
2. Walking and stopping on command.
3. Playing 'Traffic Lights' using a green and a red bean bag. Green means 'go', red means 'stop'.
4. Walking forwards, changing to walking backwards.
5. Each child collects a hoop or mat and puts it in a space.
6. Walking around their own hoop or mat forwards and backwards.
7. Walking anywhere in the room not touching the hoops or mats.
8. Walking anywhere and on command, each child stands either inside a hoop or on a mat.
9. Walking forwards around each hoop in a room.
10. Walking forwards around the room and walking backwards around the hoop or mat.
11. Walking whilst lifting the knees high.
12. Walking using big steps then little steps.
13. Practising good posture — eyes forward, toes pointing straight ahead, holding in the tummy.

Running

1. Use activities 1 to 2 on p. 38.
2. Practise changing from running to walking and vice versa.
3. Playing the game 'Catch-a-Fly', the teacher explains and then suggests which corner the 'fly' is in. The children run to that corner. The teacher keeps them moving and changing direction.
4. Practise acceleration and deceleration.
5. Vary the speed from jogging to running and back to jogging, etc.
6. Running, jogging and jogging on the spot — repeat.
7. Running whilst keeping low to the ground.
8. Choose a place to stand. On a signal, run anywhere and on another signal, return to the chosen place.
9. Running anywhere with arms in different positions.
10. Trying to run with straight legs.

Large apparatus

Try to provide the same kind of apparatus for each group as in the diagram on p. 76(A). A bench and a mat would be ideal. Where this is not possible, choose equivalent apparatus, i.e. a low gymnastic table, or a low plank suspended across two climbing frames, or a plank leaning against a climbing frame. Carry out the following tasks:

1. Walk freely in the space around the apparatus. Do not touch it.
2. In groups: walk forwards along the bench, plank, etc. and then along the mat.
3. Walk forwards along the bench and then walk backwards along the mat.
4. Walk backwards along the bench then run across the mat.
5. Walk along lifting the knees high.
6. Experiment — long steps followed by short steps, lifting the knees high.

Resilience

This is the ability to manage the body weight safely.

Bending

1. Find out together where the body bends and why it needs to bend.
2. Bend forwards and backwards.
3. Bend each joint until a crouched position has been reached and then straighten up.
4. Sit down and bend different body parts.
5. Lie down and bend different body parts.

Bouncing

1. On the spot, bend the knees and ankles before take-off, land on the toes, then transfer weight onto the whole foot, bending the knees and ankles on landing and sinking into the floor.
2. Try small jumps, landing on the spot.
3. Try small jumps, landing in various positions in the room.
4. Pretend to be bouncing a ball.

Benches

1. Walk along and step off.   Talk
2. Walk along and jump off.   about
    landings
3. Run along, jump off, sink to the floor, whilst bending the ankles, the knees and the hips.

Mats

1. Have a mat each, run and jump over it and land.
2. Curl into a ball on the mat.
3. Do a sideways curled roll.
4. Stand up, melt down onto the mat.
5. Jumping on and off the mat.
6. The teacher takes away two of the mats and the children find a mat each to sit on.

Large apparatus

Low tables, benches and mats are required. Carry out the following tasks:

1. Get onto the apparatus, step off the apparatus and 'sink' into the ground.
2. Get onto the apparatus, step off backwards and 'sink' into the ground.

Body shape

An awareness of the simple movements that can change the shape of the body should be developed, such as: 1. stretching, 2. curling, 3. shapes made using different bases and 4. moving using different body shapes. Link this theme with the theme 'Shape' suggested for use in the classroom.

Stretching

1. Stretch one arm up — both arms — the fingers and make a tall, thin shape.
2. Stretch the arms and legs wide to form a star shape.
3. Walk around the space in a tall, thin shape.
4. Walk around the space in a wide star shape.

Curling

1. Curl into a small shape (stay on feet).
2. Walk around the space in a curled shape.
3. Alternately assume thin, star and curled shapes — devising a game.

Sitting

1. Stretch out arms, hands and fingers, then curl them up.
2. Stretch out legs and toes, then curl them.
3. Curl into a ball and then 'explode' into a star shape.

Kneeling/lying

1. Try lying on the back, the front, the side and stretching into different shapes — star, thin, ball and irregular shapes or these shapes using one arm, one arm and one leg, etc.

Moving

1. With a hoop each, run around the room and on a command, curl into a ball inside the hoop. Alternate between ball, star and thin shapes and devise a game.
2. Play 'Hedgehogs and Lampposts.' 'Hedgehogs' are small and ball-shaped, whilst 'Lampposts' are tall and thin-shaped. The teacher calls 'Hedgehogs' or 'Lamposts' and the children change into that shape and move around.
3. Play 'Caterpillar' — moving along in a long stretched thin shape and then in a small, curled shape.
4. Play 'Snakes' — moving the body along without assistance from the hands or the feet.
5. 'Crouch' jump with the weight on both hands, curl the body and then the weight on both feet.
6. Jump around the room in a curled shape, then stretch high in the air.

Large apparatus

Mats

1. Move across on the knees keeping a curled shape.
2. Move across on the feet, keeping a curled-up shape.
3. Try point 1 and point 2 with a stretched shape.
4. Curl up and try a sideways roll.
5. Stretch out and try a 'roly-poly'.
6. Curl into a ball shape and try rocking.
7. Stand on one foot and hold a stretched shape.
8. Kneel on one leg and hold a stretched shape.
9. Curl up on any base — stretch out suddenly — 'surprise me!'

Benches

1. Climb on and step off.

2. Climb on, jump off and progress to a jump with the body stretched.
3. Practise moving along in a curled shape.
4. One child holds a hoop on the bench and the others curl up to go through it.
5. Practise long stretched steps.
6. Walk along in a star shape, a 'Hedgehog' shape, a 'Lamppost' shape, etc.
7. Walk as in point 6 but backwards or turning.
8. Walk making a selected shape — hands on head or on hips, or one stretched out.
9. Clap hands in front and behind.
10. Start in a 'Lamppost' shape and finish in a star shape.
11. Move along on seats, using feet and hands to propel the body.

Ropes
1. Hang in a straight shape.
2. Grip the rope and make a curled shape.
3. Hang on the rope and make different shapes with the legs.

Tasks
1. Make a wide shape somewhere on the apparatus.
2. Make a tall, thin shape, or a long, thin shape on the apparatus.
3. Try making a small, curled shape on the apparatus.
4. Try and create two different shapes on the apparatus.
5. Move around or along the apparatus, keeping curled up for most of the time.
6. Find out how often you can make a wide shape with your legs. The children must be reminded to take care when landing from the apparatus.

Travelling

Children can be made aware of the different parts of their body that can be used in order to travel. Children should also be allowed to experience travelling in different directions and on different pathways:

1. Walking in different directions, at different speeds, at different levels. Walking with different steps — long, small, on tiptoes, on heel and toe, on the heels, with feet astride and together.
2. Running in different directions at different levels and at different speeds.
3. Jumping about the room on two feet.
4. Hopping.
5. Skipping.
6. Side-slipping.
7. Galloping.
8. Leaping.
9. Travelling on hands and feet; a) face to the floor; b) back to the floor; c) side to the floor.
10. Sitting on their bottoms, using the feet to propel the body.
11. Lying on their fronts, backs and sides, using the hands to propel the body.
12. On their seats dragging the body behind, the two hands and arms move the body — like seals!
13. Repeat but use one hand and one foot.
14. Rolling, pushing and pulling and sliding.
   (The teacher should remember to ask the children to practise at different *levels* and to use different *speeds*).
15. One child gets inside a hoop and another holds the hoop against the first child's waist. One pretends he is a horse and the other, a coachman. They can travel around the room and practise stopping, accelerating and decelerating.

Apparatus

Choose arrangements that allow the children access to large surface areas — benches, planks, a long mat, table tops, etc.

Tasks

1. Practising different ways of moving along the apparatus. Get the children to think about which parts of the body they are travelling on.
2. Finding different ways of moving under and over the apparatus.
3. Using hands and feet only to travel over and along the apparatus.
4. Practising travelling with one part of the body held higher than the rest.

Fun activities
1. 'Turtle walk'. Moving around in a star shape, facing the floor.
2. 'Hanky-panky'. Holding the ankles and walking about.

Weight-bearing

Try to focus the children's attention on the parts of the body that can take their weight. Explore the parts that are most useful. For example, the children can be instructed to:

1. Walk — 'freeze' on command.
2. Run — 'freeze' on command.
3. Sit on the floor — lift legs and arms in the air.
4. Lie on fronts and lift chests, legs and arms in the air.
5. Make a bridge — facing the floor — put the weight on hands and feet.
6. Make a bridge with two hands and one foot, then two feet and one hand.
7. Face the floor — make the widest star shape possible and hold it.
8. Pretend they are a stork and stand on one foot. Then put the side of other foot behind the calf of leg.
9. 'Heel and toe'. Walk forward. The heel of new foot always touches the toe of the other foot.
10. Stand on one foot and lean forward until the body is in the shape of the letter T.
11. Place a bean bag a half metre away. Stand sideways to the bean bag and try to reach and touch it with the foot nearest. Replace the foot without wobbling!
12. Practise walking along a chalk line.
13. Practise walking around a hoop — near it but not touching it.

Mats
1. Put the weight on the lower legs.
2. Put the weight on one lower leg.
3. Put the weight on the head, feet and one hand. (Try with no hands?)
4. Walk across the mat with two hands and one foot — keep the other leg high. Try right and left feet alternately.
5. Walk across the mat with one hand and one foot.

85

6. Put the weight on the back by lying on the back and raising the legs, head and arms off the floor.
7. Put the weight on the stomach by lying face down on the floor and raising the legs, head and arms off the floor.
8. Put weight on one side of the body by lying on one side and lifting legs and head.
9. Experiment by choosing different parts to put your body weight on. Keep still on the part that you have chosen.

Apparatus

Choose apparatus with large surface areas.

Tasks

1. Practise holding a position on the apparatus, e.g. standing like a stork, making a 'bridge' or a 'star'. Seat sit (lifting legs and arms).
2. Get onto the apparatus using different parts of the body, e.g. the knees, bottom, stomach and hands.
3. Try sliding off the apparatus with the hands projecting forward.

Fun activities

1. 'Kicking donkey' — put weight on the hands and kick the feet into the air.
2. 'Threading the needle' — clasp the hands together and lift one foot through the 'loop' until hands are behind the knee.
3. 'Claps' — put weight on the hands and one foot. Lift the hands, clap and put the hands down again.
4. 'Claps' — sit down on the foor, lift the legs and clap the hands underneath the legs.

MIDDLE INFANTS

The six-year-old is probably far more capable than we expect and is certainly capable of learning quite complex motor skills if given the opportunity. Such children need a stimulating environment and time for practising skills. The average child at the end of the second year should be able to:

1. Hop skilfully on each foot, on the spot, and moving forwards.
2. Gallop.
3. Skip.

4. Balance on each foot for over 20 seconds.
5. Complete a sequence of crouch jumps.
6. Land from a height and control the body weight.
7. Run, leap and land with control.
8. Climb on, up and from apparatus.
9. Hang upside down from the knees from low apparatus.
10. Roll sideways in a stretched and a curled position.
11. Complete a forward roll.
12. Attempt a handstand but not balance.
13. Walk along a balance beam without falling off.
14. Jump to a height of 20 cm.
15. Take the weight on the head and hands for two seconds (headstand).
16. Remain still on different parts of the body.
17. Hang on the ropes with two hands.
18. Crouch jump along a bench.

At the beginning of the year, it is advisable, particularly after the long summer holidays, to recap on the previous year's work. Special attention should be given to the practice of managing the body weight successfully and safely. Suggested themes are as follows:

1. Resilience;
2. Travelling;
3. Weight-bearing;
4. Balancing;
5. Rolling and rocking.

Resilience

Bouncing

1. Bouncing on the spot. Re-teach the necessity to 'sink into the floor', 'to catch your weight', 'to bend the ankles, knees and hips'.
2. Use hoops to bounce in and out of, with two feet together — forwards, backwards, sideways, with a turn.

Jumping

1. Run in the room, leap into the air and *practise landings*.
2. Run and jump over a hoop. One-footed take-off and landing.
3. Run and jump over small mats.

4. Practise a two-footed take-off and landing, then a one-footed take-off and landing.
5. Practise jumping from benches and landing on two feet.
6. Practise jumping over planks and benches.
7. Practise jumping over each other — one child curls up in a kneeling position on the floor. Take off on one foot and land on two feet.

Running

1. Practise running at speed and stopping.
2. Run and on the command 'freeze', holding that position.
3. Run and on command, jump in the air and land.

Apparatus

Choose items that children can jump down from — nests of tables (of different heights), benches, low planks, climbing frames.

Tasks

1. Practise jumping off the apparatus.
2. Practise landing on one foot after the other.
3. Try to jump off backwards.

Travelling

To extend the work started in reception class, the first to the sixth activities p. 84 from the reception class syllabus should be revised and repeated. Use these activities as an introduction to the lesson. Get the children to:

1. Experiment — try moving on three parts of the body, then try moving on two parts of the body. Suggest the different parts that can be used to *propel* the body.
2. Use a long, thin shape to roll and travel.
3. Use a curled-up shape to roll sideways and travel. *Practise some of these activities* very slowly (like a slow-motion film). Practise them very quickly (like one of the early Charlie Chaplin films). Experiment with acceleration and deceleration and remember to use words that will enrich the children's language.
4. Practise travelling with different parts of the body leading, e.g. foot, knee, head, seat, etc.

5. Move along on the back with the feet in the air.
6. Travel like a frog, a dog, a rabbit, a seal, a giraffe, a snake.
7. Travel like a robot.

Tasks performed on the apparatus

1. Practise different ways of travelling on feet and hands only.
2. Use benches and planks to practise travelling by pushing, rolling, and sliding.
3. Practise travelling upside down on a low bar or ladder.
4. Practise travelling by pencil-rolling along benches, planks and padded tables and boxes.

The gymnastic theme 'travelling' enriches the classroom work on transport as there are various links betweem them.

Movement links between 'travelling' and 'transport'

1. Traffic: Work on speeds and directions.
2. Revolution: Work on revolving and rotating.
3. Power: Work on weight and forces.

Work on speeds and directions

1. Stopping and starting.
2. Acceleration and deceleration.
3. Reversing.
4 Moving right and left.
5. Moving up and down. (Upstairs and downstairs on a double-decker bus.)

Revolving

1. Turning on the spot to the right and left.
2. Using a hoop to practise going round to the right and left.
3. Rolling on the floor (pencil roll) to practise revolving like a wheel.
4. Making curved pathways.
5. Walking in any direction and on command, turning round once and walking in any direction again.
6. Using quoits as steering wheels — practising turning the quoit to move right and left and all the way round.
7. Circling the hands at the wrists and the arms at the shoulders.
8. Spinning around on the seat and on the tummy.

Power

1. Practising strengthening actions, tensing the muscles, pressing, pulling and pushing individually.
2. Practising pulling in twos (sitting legs outstretched).
3. Practising pulling in twos (standing with outstretched hands).
4. Practising pulling in twos, one behind the other.
5. Facing a partner, putting the palms together and pushing.
6. One partner stands and exerts strength, the other tries to move the partner.

Fun ideas

1. Trains — two together, four together, six together.
2. Moving together with identical movements (notion of two wheels).
3. Moving together extended to four people (notion of four wheels).
4. Wheel patterns — moving around an axle/axis.
5. Traffic lights — using red, yellow and green bean bags. Move on green, slow down on yellow, stop on red.

Weight-bearing

Supporting the body weight. Repeat activities one to thirteen from the reception class syllabus (p. 85) then add the following:

1. Stand on one leg, lift a bean bag with the toes of the right foot and put the bean bag near the left foot. Repeat with the other foot.
2. Try to balance on each foot in turn with the eyes closed.
3. Stand on the right foot and put the left leg and both arms in a particular shape. Repeat with the right foot.
4. Stand on one foot. Experiment and bend forwards, backwards and sideways.
5. Kneel down with the hands on the floor. Lift one hand, lift both hands and put them back.
6. Kneel down and fall forward, using the hands to prevent total collapse.
7. Practise walking along a 2.5m skipping rope stretched along the floor. Move forwards and backwards — one foot in front/behind the other.

Fun activities

Repeat points one to four (p. 86) from the reception syllabus. The teacher suggests a part of the body to use. The children move from their seats, to their knees to their feet on command.

Apparatus

A mixture of travelling and weight-bearing.

Benches

1. Practise moving along on different parts of the body.
2. Practise moving backwards and sideways, turning on different parts of the body.
3. As points 1 and 2 but hold any one part of the body still when reaching the middle of the bench.

Planks

1. Practise sliding on different parts of the body.
2. Slide with different parts of the body leading (head, feet).
3. Slide on different parts of the body (sides, etc., with the head leading or the feet leading).
4. Hold a position halfway down the plank.

Ladders

1. Travel up and down the ladder facing front and then with the back towards the ladder.
2. Travel along the ladder facing front and facing backwards.

Climbing on climbing frame

1. Travel using hands and feet only.
2. Travel using hands and one foot only.
3. Climb up on the outside and down on the inside of the climbing frame.
4. Climb up to the top and try to travel down using hands only.

Climbing on bars

1. Try a sloth-like method of travelling. Wrap the legs around the bar, cling on with the hands and travel forwards, head leading. Come back with the feet leading.
2. Try hanging on with the legs straight and then the legs curled.

Climbing on ropes

1. Sit down. Use the arms to pull the body off the floor, except for the heels.

2. From a standing position, jump, grasp the rope and hang.
3. As for point 2 but curl the legs then stretch them.
4. Swing on the ropes.

Balancing

The ability to hold the body still on different bases. This theme leads on naturally from the previous theme. Practise walking in restricted areas:

1. Backwards, heel to toe and around a hoop.
2. Forwards and backwards, heel to toe and along a skipping rope.
3. Practise walking on the heels, toes and the sides of the feet.

Benches

Place with the balance side up. Children should be encouraged to move slowly to control their movements.

1. Move forwards slowly, stop at the end and make a controlled jump off the end onto a mat.
2. Do not progress to other activities until point one has been achieved. Then practise walking backwards and sideways.
3. Experiment with different types of steps — heel and toe, sideways steps and on tiptoes.
4. Use different arm positions — hands on hips, hands on heads, arms above the head, arms outstretched, arms folded, etc.
5. Clap the hands in front and behind.
6. Balance a bean bag on the head, shoulder, etc.
7. Move to the centre of the bench and try to balance on one leg in a particular shape. Set challenges, e.g. 'Stop in the middle and make your knee touch your chin', or 'Pick up a bean bag, then put it down again'.

Obstacles

1. One child can hold a hoop in different positions and at different heights and then progress to stepping through the hoop — forwards, backwards and sideways and then to stepping into and then out of the hoop.
2. Try to roll a ball along the bench with your hands.
3. Try tossing the ball up and catching it as you walk.

Shoulder standing

Teach the children to balance on their shoulders. Get them to lie down with arms by their sides and then to bend the arms at the elbows so that the lower arms are vertical, spread the hands out, lift the legs and lower body high into the air, press down on to the floor with the upper arms and support the body at waist level on the hands. *Try and keep still and do not wobble!*

Handstand

Teach the children the basic essentials:

1. Hands flat on the floor palms down.
2. Hands shoulder-width apart.
3. Fingers spread and pointing forwards.
4. Arms and elbows straight.
5. Put the weight on the hands, kick up the legs, one leading.
6. Shoulders should move forward but not past the vertical.

Headstand

1. Kneel on the mat.
2. Put the hands flat on the mat, the shoulder-width apart.
3. Put the forehead on the mat ahead of the hands. (The hands and forehead should be placed to form the three points of an equilateral triangle.)
4. Equal pressure should be placed on head and hands.
5. Push down on the hands and head.
6. Walk the feet forwards towards the hands.
7. Lift the feet and legs slowly. Keep pushing down.

Apparatus

Only use pieces of apparatus that provide a surface which can be balanced on!

1. Use a crash mat on which the children can practise a head-stand with the teacher supervising.
2. Practise holding positions of balance on the surfaces provided.

Rocking and rolling

Rolling is an essential skill in gymnastics. Rocking activities are a helpful pre-activity that lead into rolling and help children to gain confidence in transferring their weight from one part of the body to another.

Use individual mats wherever possible and:

1. Practise stretching and curling — staying on the feet.
2. Practise crouching and 'tucking up' on the mat — staying on the feet.
3. Practise crouch jumps across the mat and around the mat with the head tucked in with the weight on the hands and then on the feet.
4. Rock from side to side in a tucked position (on their sides).
5. Rock from shoulders to seats in a tucked position (on their backs).
6. Experiment — rock on any part of the body.
7. Roly-poly across the mat.
8. Do a sideways tucked roll across the mat.

Forward roll

1. Place the hands flat on the floor slightly ahead of the feet.
2. Tuck the chin onto the chest.
3. Look backwards through the legs.
4. Use both feet to push the body forward.
5. Try to keep the body rounded with the knees tucked into the chest and the heels close to seat.
6. Roll gently — onto the shoulders — the back — the seat — the feet.

N.B. The head and neck should not support the weight of the body at any time.

Apparatus

1. Use benches to practise a sideways roly-poly.
2. Use mats for sideways tucked rolls.
3. Use mats for forward rolls.
4. Use movement tables to lean off (with the weight on the stomach) onto two hands, pushing forwards, followed by a tuck and roll on the mat.
5. Use climbing frames in a similar way.

TOP INFANTS

If the children have followed a comprehensive programme for the two years prior to their third year at school, they should be almost capable of carrying out most gymnastic skills, allowing for strength and height. At the end of the year a child should be able to:

1. Run at speed and stop suddenly.
2. Jump from a two-footed take-off position.
3. Run, leap and experience flight.
4. Balance on one foot for longer than 30 seconds.
5. Travel with bounding leaps from one foot to another.

Some children should also be able to:

1. Complete a handstand with both legs held high (5 per cent).
2. Complete a roll backwards, both straight over the head and tucked (20 per cent).
3. Attempt a handstand. Ten per cent should be able to balance.
4. Climb a rope (40 per cent).
5. Complete a somersault over a bar and/or between two ropes (40 per cent).
6. Have the ability to complete 'shoulder standing'.
7. Roll backwards over one shoulder.
8. Roll forwards in a curled position.
9. Complete a handstand with at least one leg held high.
10. Lie on the tummy and touch head with feet.
11. Achieve flight from apparatus with a controlled landing.
12. Roll on the apparatus.
13. Balance on small parts of the body.
14. Hang in different positions on bars and ropes.
15. Swing on a rope in a controlled manner.

It is advisable, after the long summer holiday, to check that the children have remembered how to use their bodies resiliently. Teachers are advised to spend at least two weeks on bouncing, jumping and running exercises, etc.

Themes in this section include:

1. Rocking and rolling.
2. Rolling and somersaults.
3. Jumping.
4. Flight.
5. Hanging and swinging.
6. Integrated themes.

Rocking and rolling

1. Revise the previous year's work on rocking and rolling.
2. Teach the forward roll again and use the associated large apparatus activities.
3. Teach the backward roll.

Teaching points

Get the children to use mats.

1. Clasp the fingers behind the neck.
2. Spread the elbows sideways.
3. Crouch down on two feet with the back to the mat.
4. Sit down quickly — rock — tuck the knees up to chin, tuck and roll, taking the weight on the upper arms.

Progression

1. Take up a tucked position — weight on the feet and the back towards the mat.
2. Bend the arms at the elbows with the palms facing towards ceiling and the fingertips towards the shoulders.
3. Tip onto the heels, sit down, tuck the knees up, and with the palms on the floor, push on the hands and roll over.

This activity must be completed with speed and flow to achieve the necessary momentum.

Rolling activities on mats

1. Roll forward with one leg extended.
2. Roll with the legs crossed, forwards and backwards.
3. Roll forwards with the legs stretched wide.
4. Roll backwards with the legs stretched wide.
5. Roll forwards, turn and go straight into a backward roll.
6. Roly-poly.

Benches

1. Place a mat along the bench, *roll* along the bench — a forward roll, then a backward roll and a roly-poly.
2. With a mat along the bench and one on the floor beside it, forward roll over the bench. (The feet on one side, the hands the other side.)

N.B. These activities are ideas and suggestions but should *never* be made compulsory.

Movement tables

1. Roll on the top choosing a sideways or forward direction.
2. Lie across the table, reach down with the hands, tuck the head in and slowly slide into a forward roll. Or, jump off the table and roll on the mat. (These are possible suggestions.)

Rolling and somersaults

Add somersault activities to theme 1. The children will have become used to using their hands to grip ropes, ladders and bars when practising hanging exercises whilst in the middle infants. However, the hand grips are often the key to performing successful somersaults.

Progression

1. Climbing in and out of the wall bars. (Make the children become aware of what their hands are doing.)
2. Coming off the wall bars on the hands with the feet following.
3. Task: Practise rolling or somersaulting on the apparatus *or on the floor* saying, 'If you need help, ask me' or 'You choose where you want to work.'
4. Practise rolling — somersaulting over a bar.

Teaching points

1. The bar should rest along the top leg joint and the feet should be off the floor.
2. The weight should be transferred to the stomach.
3. The hand grip should be with the thumb forwards and the fingers backwards.
4. Tuck the head under the bar, move the weight along the legs, tuck the legs to start the curling momentum, pull on the hands and roll/somersault around.

Reverse somersaults on the bars

1. Sit on the bar using a grip with the fingers forward and the thumb backwards.
2. Pull hard on the hands and arms and slip the weight backwards until both knees are hooked over the bar.
3. Push the knees forward, follow with the bottom, let go with

the knees and push with one foot on the bar until hanging up-side down in the reverse position. Drop off from the hands.

Reverse somersaults with the bar lower

1. Reach up with two hands to grasp the bar.
2. Jump to bring both legs in the tucked position up to chest.
3. Bring the legs through the space between the arms, hang and then complete the somersault.

Reverse somersaults on the ropes

1. Practise hanging with the legs making different shapes.
2. Practise jumping into the tucked position. Grip the rope with the hands at shoulder height and pull the arms into a bent position.
3. As for point 2 but on the jump, pull hard on the hands, keep the arms bent and throw the head and hips upwards and backwards and wrap the legs around the rope.
4. After many turns at point 3, let go with legs, tuck up and complete the somersault.
5 Either let go or jump back to the starting position.

N.B. Children who do not feel confident should be allowed to use the mats on the floor to carry out the task.

Jumping

Practise simple leaping and jumping activities as introductory activities.

1. Run and leap as far as you can.
2. Run and leap as high as you can.
3. Try with a different foot leading the leap.
4. Practise jumping on two feet to 65cm; left to right; right to left; two feet and land on left foot; right foot to 65cm; left foot to two feet.
5. From a standing start, jump in different directions.
6. Leap over objects such as hoops, small mats or other children.
7. Jump and turn.

Benches

1. Walk and jump off on to a mat.
2. Try the variations in points 1 to 4 along the bench.

3. Try variations in points 1 to 4 off the bench.
4. Practise jumping over the bench, two feet together, right to left foot, left to right foot, etc.

Mats

Practise jumping over the mat.

Other apparatus

Practise jumping down from any climbing apparatus or movement table. *Emphasise* good relaxed landings.

Flight

This is a natural progression from jumping. Try all the activities practised in the section on jumping but *emphasise* what the body is doing in the air.

1. Leap as high as you can.
2. Leap high and stretch your arms.
3. Push off the floor and reach to the sky. Make a shape whilst you are in the air.

Hanging and swinging

A number of hanging activities will have been practised during the previous two years. Now that the children have more confidence, proceed to develop their skill:

1. Practise hanging on ropes, climbing frames, ladders and bars:
   1. Hang with the arms bent and extended.
   2. Hang with the legs straight, toes pointed and the legs tucked in.
   3. Practise touching the bar, rope, etc., with different parts of the body whilst hanging, e.g.. knee, toe, soles of feet.
   4. Hang upside down from the knees.
   5. Try hanging from one hand and one knee.
   6. Try hanging from one hand (at a low height).
2. Practise moving along from rope to rope using legs and hands.
3. Practise moving along underneath horizontal ladders, poles

and bars using the hands and the legs with the back facing the floor.
4. Practise moving along a bar using the hands only.
5. Practise hanging upside down from the knees on ladders, poles, bars and climbing frames and swinging the body from left to right.
6. Practise swinging on one rope in a tucked position.
7. Practise swinging on two ropes in a tucked position.

Integrated themes

When children become proficient at gymnastic skills, it is enjoyable for them to have tasks to work to, i.e. *set limitations*. Arrange some apparatus and ask the children to move about on their hands and feet only. Or ask them to perform *set tasks* — to get off the apparatus feet first or to try and move about the apparatus on the knees (lower leg) for as long as possible.

Curling and stretching

1. Curl up and get on the apparatus and stretch out to get off the apparatus.
2. Curl up and remain in this position whilst moving on, along, over and off the apparatus.

Feet together

Move along keeping the feet together all the time whilst moving on, along, through, under and off the apparatus.

Directions

Get on to the apparatus, move along by turning — go over and through the apparatus by turning. Get on forwards, get off backwards, etc.

Change of speed

When you are on the apparatus, sometimes move very slowly, also, choose a safe place to move quickly.

Different ways of getting on to the apparatus

1. Start by lying down and pull yourself on to the apparatus.
2. Use a different part of the body to get on to the apparatus each time.
3. Get on backwards.

4. Get on so that the hands are the last part of the body to leave the floor, etc.

Ideas

1. Make different stretched shapes on the apparatus.
2. Find a place to hang and then try swinging from side to side.
3. Get on the apparatus with the same part of the body as the one you get off with.
4. Show three balancing positions on three different parts of your body.
5. Climb to the top of the frame on the outside and climb down on the inside.
6. Go over and under as many places as you can.
7. Try and keep your back to the apparatus all the time.

The teacher needs to check by making such comments as, for example:

'Which part of your body did you use to get on to your apparatus Paul?'
'I did not see you choose three balance positions!'
'Let us all watch Susan. She has found six different stretched shapes.'
'Claire, I didn't like that landing. Your feet were not together and you did not sink into the ground!'
'Good, Simon, you have tried very hard to do well', etc.

REFERENCES

1. Wetton, P. *Child Education* (Scholastic Publications, 1983).

USEFUL READING

J. Learmouth & K. Whitaker (1976) *Movement in Practice* (Schofield & Sims, Huddersfield, 1976).
E. Mauldon & J. Layson *Teaching Gymnastics* (McDonald and Evans, London, 1980).
Kent County Council Education Committee, *Teaching Gymnastics in the Primary School*.

6

Games in the Infant School

A dictionary definition of games would probably read 'organised play according to rules; play, amusement; sport'. A better definition of games in the infant school, however, would undoubtedly be 'organised play in order to promote motor skill learning and enjoyment, according to simple rules'. Thus our long-term aim in teaching games in this age group should be to begin the process that will enable a child to develop a competency base that will eventually allow him to enjoy an active and healthy adult life, both at work and at leisure. The aim in the short term, however, is to provide a sequential programme of games activities within a well-balanced PE curriculum that will meet the needs of the child's total development.

So, how can we begin to put a structured games programme into the curriculum? First of all, it would seem important to consider the content of such a programme. But before this, perhaps I should suggest that most teachers are more concerned with either the method they should use or the 'management constraints' that exist within the school.

Let us consider the 'management constraints'. The most important of these would seem to be the hall timetable. Therefore, the first task is to clear a space on the timetable for games in the hall. Yes, it can be done! Leaving spaces on the timetable for flexible arrangements for teachers to use the hall does not always work. Teachers need a recognised timetable slot. There are several ways to achieve this if teachers are willing to be positive. It can be painful, since change means altering a set teaching pattern, but it can be done. First of all try the obvious and timetable some of the 'flexi-time'. Secondly, take 15 minutes each, instead of 30 minutes, for games. Cut singing practice or practising for assembly by 5 minutes, or site the TV in another place, or take the 15 minutes before setting out the dinner tables.

This all sounds swashbuckling and severe, but if the entire staff is willing to talk the situation through and decide where the priorities lie for the children, then it can be achieved. Failing this, then do something even better and set aside part of your own personal class timetable for a period outdoors.

The next most important constraint is probably the PE store. Why not have a spring clean? Why not work together as a staff when you do this, so that someone's favourite piece of equipment is not sited on the top shelf? Try and provide a clear route to the games equipment so that it is readily accessible to both children and staff. Where possible, store the equipment in containers with handles, or, better still, on trolleys. This makes the management of the lesson so much simpler and therefore so much easier to contemplate.

I would then suggest that each teacher invests in a pair of trainers or similar footwear and if you are to teach outdoors — a thick jumper. (If we are to be honest, we are the ones who do not want to go outside, not the children!)

Having considered ways to make the management easier, it would probably help now to consider the methods of teaching games. Although teachers are knowledgeable about content, many are no longer confident about teaching games. They feel unsure and worried that what they are doing will be classed as 'old-fashioned', or will be frowned upon as 'not suitable'. My answer to this is, do it your own way. It is far better for the children to do it your way than not to do it at all! Children must be active, preferably in the fresh air and, at this stage in their lives, they need the assistance of the class teacher to help them not only develop their physical games skills, but also to help them cope with their emotional and moral development. There is a suggestion too that as children now find fewer and fewer safe spaces to play outside school hours, teachers may be the last source for passing on some of the traditional games which are part of British culture. Teachers are also in the unique position of being able to teach their children how to play the games from other cultures and indeed to guide children into playing harmoniously with each other.

. Having decided to 'do it', help yourself by starting with short periods of activity and gradually build up to a longer lesson over a period of weeks. Two periods of 15 minutes each week are better than one lasting 30 minutes when children are learning skills. It must be remembered too, that 15 minutes is quite long enough for children in the reception class.

In the early stages, the basic pattern of the lesson should be a general warm-up until the children are 'puffing', followed by teaching, learning, or practising a skill and then a concluding class activity. Here are a few examples, graded for children as they develop their skill and expertise:

EXAMPLE ONE

Warm-up
Aim: To teach large ball activities:

1. Free running around the yard getting the children to stop and freeze on command.
2. Jumping on the spot with feet together.

Learning skill

1. Hold the ball in both hands, drop it, then pick it up.
2. Roll the ball along the ground, chase after it, then pick it up.
3. Hold the ball and run as fast as possible.

Conclusion

End with a class game.
N.B. It is easier to manage a lesson if only one type of apparatus is taken outside each time, particularly with the younger children. However, when children have become used to working with different kinds of apparatus, it is possible to allow an element of choice.

EXAMPLE TWO

Aim: To teach children how to kick a large ball.

Warm-up

1. A chasing game.
2. Free choice from the apparatus trolley.

Learning skills

1. Tap the ball with the inside of the foot.
2. Take the ball for a 'walk' with the feet propelling the ball.
3. Stand and kick the ball. Use the instep.
4. Run up to and kick the ball.
5. Dribble the ball, kick the ball.

Conclusion

In small groups, practise shooting between 'goal-posts' (use skittles). Other methods may be used as children grow older.

EXAMPLE THREE

Aim: To give practise in ball skills.

Warm-up

1. A class game.
2. Jumping activities.

Stations

Create a circuit of five activities each connected with a particular set of skills. For example: 1. Handling large balls, or 2. Foot skills with a large ball, or 3. Multi-skills for evaluation purposes. If the activity is 'Handling large balls' — five groups of six children could:

1. Practise throwing and catching in twos.
2. Practise pat-bouncing the ball and count the number of successive pats.
3. Throw the ball high, let it bounce and catch it.
4. Hold hoops in the air and those without could practise throwing the ball through the hoop and catching it.
5. Practise throwing the ball underarm to hit a box or skittle.

Conclusion

A quiet class activity.

EXAMPLE FOUR

Aim: To teach the game of 'Circular Rounders'. (Choose a game, analyse it, teach the necessary skills, then play it.)

Warm-up

Run, with control, around the area, run clockwise and anti-clockwise.

Learning skills

1. Throw and catch a ball in twos underarm.
2. Count how many times you can throw and catch the ball in 20 seconds.
3. Throw and catch the ball five times. One person holds the ball, the other runs around their partner and then back to his place. Repeat.
4. Arrange the class in four lines. One person with the ball stands two metres away facing them. He throws the ball to the first person in the line, who throws it back, runs around the thrower and runs to the back of the line. Each person takes a turn.

Circular passing rounders

Divide the class into four teams. Each team forms one side of a square facing inwards. One person from each team stands in the middle with a large ball. The person in the middle throws the ball to each person in their team in turn. The last to have a turn runs around the outside of the other teams and back to the first place in their line. The game continues until each player has had a turn.

. It is most essential throughout all of these activities to consider the content of the games curriculum. Remember the main aims, which are learning skills and promoting fitness within a social and moral framework. It is easy to list the activities that are necessary if our children are to be physically fit and to list the skills in the progressive order in which they can be learned. It is not so easy to list the social and moral attitudes and skills which will be learned *en passant*. The teaching of games skills, therefore, should be planned with a number of basic principles in mind.

1. Structure the lessons so that there is maximum participation for each child.
2. Plan so that every child can do well. Success is of paramount importance.
3. Make the lessons fun!
4. If there is to be an increase in skill, many many repetitions are necessary.
5. Put the emphasis on learning by doing. Keep teacher talk to a minimum.

Skills implicit in all primary games can be classified into two main areas — locomotor skills and manipulative skills.

LOCOMOTOR SKILLS

Walking, running and jumping are examples of such skills.

Walking

This is a known skill that can be used to help children learn many strategies at a slower tempo than running.

Activities based on walking

1. Walk slowly; walk quickly; change on the teacher's signal.
2. Walk on heels; walk on toes; change on the teacher's signal.
3. Take long strides; take small steps; change on the teacher's signal.
4. Walk anywhere, turn on teacher's signal and walk in another direction.
5. Walk on the lines of the playground.
6. Walk backwards; walk sideways, carry out slip steps.
7. Walk, then on the teacher's signal, turn a complete circle and carry on walking.

There are many more activities based on walking which will encourage the children to be aware of *what* their legs, feet and bodies can do, *how* their legs and feet can move and, most importantly, *where* they can move. The signals given by the teacher are crucial in these activities as they encourage listening skills. Also, as the children practise the activities at a slower tempo, they will become orientated within the area in which they are working. In these elementary practices lie the fundamental beginnings and responses to all known games.

Running

This activity should involve a slight leaning of the body. The knees should be lifted and the arms should be bent at the elbows and swing forwards and backwards from the shoulders. The children should be encouraged to push against the ground with the balls of the feet and to keep their heads up and their eyes looking forward.

Activities based on running

1. Choose your own spot on the floor and remember it.
2. Run anywhere and on the signal, return to original spot.
3. Run anywhere. On the signal, return to your own spot and jump up and down until told to stop.
4. Run anywhere and on the signal, bend down and touch the floor. Then continue running.
5. Run with long steps, then tiny steps, lifting the knees higher, etc.

A very important games skill, which is often neglected, is that of stopping. Encourage the children to keep their feet apart, to bend their knees to absorb the shock of stopping and to lower their bodies slightly over their feet.

Jumping

Younger children do not find it easy to jump forward from a standing position and are not always co-ordinated enough to be able to run and jump successfully. Some practices can be suggested, however, which will help them to strengthen their joints ready to achieve force at take-off and absorb their own weight on landing.

Activities based on jumping

1. Practise small jumps on the spot, bending the hips, knees and ankles.
2. Jump on the spot with the feet together. Sink into the floor.
3. Jump on the spot and land with feet apart.
4. Try to jump higher.
5. Jump in the air with one arm stretched high.
6. Try to move around the space jumping and landing with both feet.

Games for developing locomotor skills may be chosen from the following list:

'Grandmother's footsteps' (any age)

The children stand across the room from the teacher, who stands with her back to them. The children try to creep quietly towards the teacher, who turns round from time to time. Any child seen moving must return to the start. The aim is to try and touch the teacher.

'What time is it Mr. Wolf?' (reception class)

The children walk behind the teacher. When she turns round, everybody stops. The children ask, 'What time is it Mr. Wolf?' The teacher chooses a time, e.g. nine o' clock and turns round. The children continue to follow her. When the teacher says 'Dinner-time', the children run away and the teacher tries to catch them.

'Tom Tiddler's ground' (middle and top infants)

The children line up with their backs to the wall and face across the room. The teacher stands in the middle of the room. She is 'Tom Tiddler'. The children try to run across the room without the teacher touching them. If a child is touched, he joins the teacher and helps to touch the other children crossing next time. The last person to be touched becomes 'Tom Tiddler'.

'Simon says' (any age)

The children are asked to complete certain actions. If the action is prefaced by 'Simon Says', the children can complete the task. If they complete a task without the prefix, they are 'caught out'. Examples could include 'Simon says jump on the spot!' or 'Simon says bend down!' If the teacher simply says 'Stand up!' anyone doing so is caught out.

'Statues' (any age)

The children are told to run anywhere. Then the teacher directs them to make a certain shape such as a tree, a sleeping lion, a prickly bush, a monster, etc. The children must obey and remain completely still.

'Back to back' (reception)

The children run around and when the teacher calls 'now!' the children must find a partner and stand back to back.

'Calls' (any age)

The teacher calls out certain movement ideas such as 'walk like an elephant', or 'run like a cat', or 'move like a snake', or 'tiptoe through the puddle', etc. At any time she can call 'glue'. The children must 'freeze' in that position. Anyone still moving is caught out.

'Lumps' (top infants)

The children run around and when the teacher issues a directive, the children respond. Examples of commands are 'Get into groups of three people!, or ' Stand alone', or 'Get into a group of twenty-nine people!' (or however many are in the class).

Circles (middle and top infants)

The class is asked to get into circles of six. One child is selected to go first. The first child touches the second, who runs round the outside of the circle and back to her place. The second child touches a third, who also runs round the outside of the circle. When everyone has had a turn, the children raise their hands and the game has ended.

MANIPULATIVE SKILLS

It is the manipulative skills, however, which form a very important group of skills in teaching games and all-round movement competency. Basically, these skills consist of throwing, catching, kicking, rebounding and striking. It is through using different pieces of equipment such as balls of different sizes and shapes, bats of different sizes and shapes, quoits, bean bags, etc., in throwing, catching, kicking, striking and rebounding, that children begin to develop their manual dexterity, their hand-eye and foot-eye co-ordination and become competent in handling those objects that provide the basis for the more specialised games skills in later years. Learning skills is like most, if not all, learning processes, a series of stages, introduced at the correct developmental level, which must be continuous and cumulative and therefore teachers will know that the children must be introduced to each stage in the correct order.

What follows is a suggested syllabus for games in the infant school. There are three sections, one each for the reception class and middle and top infants. Each section consists of lists of activities and games which are considered suitable for each age group and which are presented in sequential order. Most of the activities are suitable for both indoor and outdoor lessons, but teachers are reminded again of the value of exercise in the fresh air! Teachers are also reminded that if lessons take place outdoors, it is a good idea to alternate activities between static and dynamic practices.

LOCOMOTOR SKILLS — WITH THE RECEPTION CLASS

Reception class children can be introduced to the locomotor skills and play the games suggested earlier in the chapter before being introduced to small apparatus.

MANIPULATIVE SKILLS

A good way to introduce the younger children to manipulative skills activities is through the use of bean bags. Bean bags are soft and easy to handle and do not roll away when dropped! Small fingers are also more able to clutch a bean bag than a ball, which is less flexible.

Bean bag activities

1. Balance the bag on your palm and walk around the room.
2. Balance the bag on the back of your hand and walk around the room.
3. Hold the bag in your right hand and run forwards, then backwards. Repeat with the left hand.
4. Put the bag on the floor, jump over it, then pick it up. Repeat.
5. Balance the bag on different parts of the body such as the head, shoulder, back, etc.

The following activities are carried out with partners:

1. Sit or stand two metres away from your partner. Practise tossing the bag gently to your partner.
2. Stand back to back. Pass the bean bag over your head to your partner. Pass the bag under your partner's legs. Pass it around the sides of your bodies.
3. Slide the bag across the floor to your partner — two metres away.

Game: 'Bean bag scatter'

The apparatus consists of a basket containing different coloured bean bags. Divide the class into four colour groups — red, green, blue and yellow. Identify a corner of the room for each colour. The teacher scatters the bean bags all over the room. The children run and pick up their colour of bean bag and put them in their colour corner. Get the children to count them and make it competitive by saying 'See which group can be first to collect all their colour of bean bag.'

Large ball activities

Try and help reception class children to be 'ball happy' by introducing them to low challenge activities so that all the children experience success.

Hand-eye skills (1)

1. Hold the ball in two hands, then only in the right hand, then only in the left hand.
2. Roll the ball, using two hands, from the waist, over the chest, under the chin, and back to waist again.
3. Roll the ball down one leg and back to the waist.
4. Roll the ball down the other leg and back to the waist.
5. Roll the ball up to your chin and around your neck.
6. Experiment by trying to roll the ball over every part of your body.
7. Stand with the legs apart, bend the knees, roll the ball around the feet, between the legs — make a figure of eight?
8. Sit down. Roll the ball along the outside of the legs then behind the back and return to the start.
9. Hold the ball in two hands. Run as fast as you can.
10. Hold the ball under one arm. Run as fast as you can.
11. Try and hold the ball under the chin, with the arm bent at the elbow, behind the knee, balanced at the ankle — use your foot to hold the ball and lift the leg high.
12. Can you balance the ball on the back of your hand? Can you balance the ball on the back of your neck? Can you balance the ball on the tips of your fingers?

Game

Arrange the class into four lines, each assigned a different colour and standing one behind the other. Give a large ball to the first person in each line.

1. Pass the ball with both hands to the person behind you. When the last person receives the ball he/she runs with the ball to the front of the line. Repeat until everyone has had a turn at the front of the line.
2. Use the same formation. Stand with the legs apart. Bend down and look through the legs. Pass the ball between the legs to the person behind.
3. Use the same formation. Pass the ball over your head to the person behind.

Foot-eye skills (1)

1. Put first the left foot, then the right foot on top of the ball without the ball moving.
2. Hold the ball between the knees, the ankles, the instep. Try and walk with the ball between the feet without dropping it.
3. Use the toes, then the insteps of the feet to tap the ball forward. Keep the ball near to you.
4. Place the ball in a stationary position. Jump over it.
5. Use your feet to take the ball for a walk anywhere in the area. Keep the ball near to you.
6. Take the ball for a walk, using your feet only, around a hoop or a mat or an obstacle.

Game

Half the class have a ball and the other half are without one. Get the children to try and keep or gain possession of the ball.

Hand-eye skills (2) (overarm throwing — stage one)

The most difficult skill to teach is probably overarm throwing. Younger children will probably not have reached a stage in the first year in the infant school where they have enough arm strength or bodily co-ordination to be able to do this. Nevertheless the process or pattern of development should be started. Teachers might like to start by using bean bags before introducing the children to large balls. The four-year-old usually tosses a ball with two hands and in an underarm motion. This is a very important and necessary first stage. Children should not be encouraged to throw for distance or to another person, since this can cause them to overbalance. They need to concentrate on thrusting the ball away from themselves, tossing the ball against a wall or some netting. Children should be given large, brightly coloured, beach balls or sponge balls and plenty of practice!

Other activities to increase hand/arm strength

1. A two-handed toss into a space. The children watch the ball and on the teacher's command, run and pick it up.
2. A two-handed toss upwards towards the sky. The children watch the ball drop. On the teacher's command, they run and pick it up.
3. Two hands behind the ball on the floor. The children push the ball until it rolls away. They watch it, and on the teacher's command they run and pick it up.

Game: 'Charlie over the water'

The class join hands in a circle. One child is 'Charlie' and stands in the middle holding a ball. The children skip around the circle singing:

'Charlie over the water,
Charlie over the sea
Charlie caught a blackbird
But he can't catch me!'

On the word 'me', the children drop hands and run anywhere in the room. At the same time, 'Charlie' throws the ball in the air, lets it drop, catches it and then says 'stop'. 'Charlie' rolls the ball towards a child. If it touches the child, that child is the new 'Charlie'. If he misses, he is 'Charlie' again. If he misses more than once, the teacher should choose a new 'Charlie'.

A variation is to have six children in the centre of the circle, each with a ball. The other children skip in a circle until the teacher says 'stop!' The circle of children drop hands and stand still. The six children roll their balls to try and touch a child in the circle. If they are successful, they exchange places. If not, they stay inside the circle.

Hand-eye skills (3) (overarm throwing — stage two)

A bean bag or a small sponge ball is needed for each child. Introduce a one-handed underarm toss with a bean bag, a small sponge ball or any small soft ball. The activities in stage one can be repeated. The children will begin to rotate their bodies and should now be encouraged to shift their body weight from the back foot to the front foot as they throw. Accuracy and distance are not important at this stage. Children should be encouraged to try and stand sideways, right-handed children with the left shoulder facing the way the item is to be tossed and the left-handed children with the opposite shoulder facing.

1. Throw the bean bag ahead of you into a space.
2. Count. Have five turns. Have five more turns. Watch where your bean bag lands.
3. Throw a small ball ahead of you into a space.
4. Have five turns. Have five more turns. Watch where your ball goes.

Game. Arrange the class into a circle. Give each child a bean bag. Three children stand in the centre of the circle. Each child

115

in the circle throws their bean bag into the middle. The children then try to retrieve their bean bag, but if they are touched by one of the three children in the middle they must join them.

Hand-eye skills (4) (aiming)

The equipment consists of one bean bag per child, a hoop shared between two children and ten obstacles.

Bean bag activities with partners.

1. Stand two metres away from your partner. Throw underarm and try and hit partner's chest; knees; feet. Take turns.
2. Throw the bean bag underarm high into the air. Let it drop on the floor and watch it all the time. The partner has to pick it up. Take turns.
3. Bend the knees, crouch down, try and throw the bean bag to your partner so that it keeps near to the ground. Aim at her knees.
4. Put a hoop on the floor between you and your partner. Practise throwing the bean bag into the hoop.
5. Practise throwing a bean bag to hit certain objects such as circles on the wall, gateposts, skittles, boxes, tree trunks, an outstretched arm, a bat held at arm's length.
6. The partner crouches down and tucks her head in. Practise throwing the bean bag over your partner. Watch where it lands. Go and pick it up. Take turns.

Game. Arrange the children in lines of four. The first child stands up, the others crouch down, the first child jumps over them and then throws the bean bag over their bodies to land on the floor in front of the second child. Repeat until everyone has had a turn.

Hand-eye skills (5) (aiming)

One large ball is needed per child.

Large balls. Make the class form a circle, give every other child a ball. The ball is then passed around the circle.

Partners

1. Roll the ball along the ground to a partner. Try rolling it with both hands, then the right hand, then the left.

2. One child turns with his back to his partner, legs astride. The ball is rolled backwards beween the legs.
3. The children run around the area with the ball held firmly in the hands. On the teacher's directive, the partners chase the children with the balls until they can touch them. They then change places.
4. One child rolls the ball ahead of her partner on the teacher's directive, the other child chases after the ball and brings it back to her partner.

Groups. In groups of four, two children stand side by side with legs astride. The other two children each roll a ball between the legs of their partners and then run and collect them. After four turns, change over.

Game. This is played in groups of four. The first child faces the other three who stand one behind the other in a line with their legs astride. The first child rolls the ball through the legs of the second and third child. The fourth child picks the ball up and runs to the front of the line. Keep going until everyone has had a turn. Do not make the game too competitive by making remarks such as 'Ah, Susan's team finished first this time,' or making it obvious who was first, second, third, fourth, and last!

Foot-eye skills (2) (kicking)

One large ball per child and seven obstacles are required. This is a striking action carried out with either foot. There are several types of kick but the one that will be of most interest will be the soccer kick. The stages are as follows:

1. The ball is placed on the floor. The body is still and prepares for the kick by flexing the foot and straightening the leg. The leg swings back and as it swings forward, it makes contact with the ball.
2. As for 1. but encourage a bent knee lift as the leg swings back, which then straightens as it swings forward to kick the ball.
3. Walk and kick the ball.
4. Run and kick the ball.

It is a good idea to arrange the children in a line along the edge of the playground or field, let them all kick at once and then retrieve their balls together. This prevents collisions!

5. Take the ball for a walk with the feet. Use the instep and the outside of the foot to tap the ball forward and keep the ball near the feet.
6. Dribble the ball (as in 5.) and on the teacher's directive, kick the ball along the ground.

Game. Practise kicking the ball between two objects — skittles, boxes, people, etc.

Hand-eye skills (6) (catching)

One large ball per child is required. This skill is much more difficult to learn than throwing because it involves a number of problems mainly concerned with co-ordination. The children have to be able to watch the object as it moves and then move into the 'line' of throw. They have to use their hands without looking at them and thus the whole process is very complicated. Children can also be fearful of the objects used. Teachers might remember what it is like to have an unidentified object flying at them from out of space — and their reaction! If the children are not to react by pulling away and turning their heads to the side, away from the ball, then the objects should be soft in the first instance and well known to the children.

Activities for catching

1. Repeated practices involving hand/arm strengthening activities with balls. Rolling, tossing, giving the ball to a partner across a reachable space, etc.
2. Practices involving watching balls rolling or being tossed into a space, rolling a ball to a partner. Emphasise the 'watching'.

Teaching Point: Hold the arms in front of the body with the palms of the hands facing and the fingers spread. When the ball makes contact with the hands, the elbows are bent quickly and the ball is pulled into the body.

N.B. It must be remembered that until the children can throw reasonably straight, then it is very difficult to teach catching! Bean bags are probably much the best object to attempt to catch in these early stages. Suggest that the thrower aims at her partner's chest.

The skills listed here for reception-class children have been presented in the order that they should be introduced to the children. Reception-class teachers know that they need to be very patient and to realise that the skills must be introduced stage by stage if learning is to take place. The teachers also know how important it is to keep up the element of fun!

RECEPTION CLASS

EVALUATION SHEET

	Co-operative	Listens to instructions	Accepted by peers	Leader?	Ball happy hands	Ball happy feet	Throwing	Dribble-feet	Aiming	Kicking	Catching	
Name:												Teacher's comments on individual children's problems or capabilities
	✔	✔			✔		✔		✔		✔	

MIDDLE INFANTS

Consult the children's evaluation sheet from the previous year's work to assess whether any of the skill-learning areas require more practice. Then begin the new year with perhaps two lessons on general loco-motor tasks and games without apparatus, followed by one or more lessons on re-learning the skills not assimilated in the reception class.

LOCOMOTOR SKILLS

Repeat the activities suggested on pages 107 and 108 and add:

Walking

1. Use any lines marked on the ground to walk along. Children can be encouraged to watch for other people coming towards

them and be ready to side-step off the line and side-step back on again.

2. Divided into twos, one child stands still, the other walks slowly or quickly on the teacher's directive in the spaces between all the standing partners. Take turns.

3. Make patterns, for example, five slow walking steps, five quick walking steps. Let the children make their own patterns. Encourage them to count aloud.

Running

1. Refer to point 2 of 'walking' and substitute running.
2. Run forwards, backwards and to one side, always facing the teacher after a signal.
3. Run anywhere forwards and on a signal, run backwards. Teachers can vary the length of time for each change to encourage listening skills.
4. With partners, one child stands behind the other and the child in front runs as fast as possible, her partner following.
5. As for point 4, but the teacher directs them to change over.
6. Practise running between two lines, five metres apart. Turn and pivot at the line.
7. As for point 6 but run backwards.
8. As for point 6 but run first with long strides, then short steps, then with the knees lifted high. The teacher should call out 'long', 'short' and then 'knees high'.

Jumping

1. Run, jump in the air and land one foot after the other.
2. Run, jump in the air and land with feet together.
3. Run, jump in the air and land with the feet apart.
4. Run and jump as high as possible.
5. Run and jump and reach with one hand as high as possible.
6. Run and jump and reach with both hands as high as possible.

Games

(See pages 109 and 110) These include 'Grandmother's footsteps', 'Tom Tiddler's ground', 'Statues' and 'Circles'.

MANIPULATIVE SKILLS

Bean bag activities

One bean bag per child is needed.

1. Balance the bean bag on different parts of the body whilst walking, then whilst running.
2. Hold the bag at the elbow, between the arm and the side, between the knees, the ankles, behind the knees and under the chin.
3. Repeat the previous point whilst walking, running, or hopping.
4. Sit down with the bean bag between the feet and then toss it into the air.
5. As for 4, but trying to toss the bean bag over the head.
6. Stand up, then tossing the bean bag into a space, watch it drop and walk to collect it. (Sometimes tossing it high in the air and sometimes as far forward as possible from the standing place.)

Bean bag circle

The class is divided into three circles and the children in each are given numbers. Number one gives the bean bag to number two who runs around the outside of the circle and then gives the bag to number three and so on until the first child has finished his turn. The first circle to complete their turns before the other circles is the winner.

Large ball activities

Hand-eye skills (7) (catching)
One large ball is needed per child and ten skittles or markers.
Repeat the hand-eye skills (1) p. 113 and then proceed.

1. Tossing the ball a little way into the air and catching it.
2. Re-teach catching skills if necessary. Get the children to watch the ball, reach out for the ball, pull the ball in to the body (flexible wrists and elbows and fingers).
3. Putting the ball on the head and catching it as it drops.

4. Dropping the ball on the floor, letting it bounce and catching it. Divide the children into twos and using both hands, practise rolling the ball across a distance of two metres to a partner.
5. Tossing the ball to a partner across a distance of two metres, aiming at the partner's chest. The partner tries to catch the ball. (Re-emphasise the teaching points for catching.)

Game

Arrange the class into groups of four. Give each group two skittles, two boxes, or two markers of some kind. Place the markers one metre apart. The first child faces the other three, who stand in a line one behind the other. The markers are placed equi-distant from the first and second child. The first child rolls the ball to the second who rolls it back to him. The first child then goes to the back of the line. The game continues until the third and fourth child in each group have completed their turn.

Large ball activities

Hand-eye skills (8) (underarm aiming — stage three throwing)

One large ball between two children, twelve bean bags, four baskets and two plastitac faces to aim at.

1. Roll the ball to a partner two metres away. Encourage the children to step on to a bent front knee as the rolling arm swings forward. (The opposite foot to the rolling arm.)
2. Throw the ball to a partner across two metres. The children should be taught to step on the opposite foot to the throwing arm, and told clearly where to aim their throw — at the chest?

Stations. Wherever possible, each child should have a large ball. Where this is not possible, substitute bean bags or any other suitable missile! Divide the class into four groups. Two groups should be aiming to hit objects.

Practise underarm throwing involving aiming at large targets. (Plastitac a large painted face on a wall or chair and try to hit the mouth). Two groups should be aiming across a short distance to place the ball into a large receptable. (Baskets or boxes with an aperture of not less than 60 cm should give the desired success.)

Large ball activities

Foot-eye skills (3) (dribbling)

Large balls and fifteen skittles or markers are needed. Repeat the foot-eye skills (2) for the reception class then add:

1. Partners. One stands still, the other children dribble the ball in and out of the spaces until the teacher gives the signal to return to their own partner. Take turns.
2. Repeat but encourage the use of both the instep and the outer part of the foot. Remind the children to use the right and left feet alternately.
3. Each child faces a partner two metres away. One child dribbles the ball around his partner and back to his own place. The ball is then kicked to the partner. Repeat.

Game. Divide the class into groups of four, five or six. Line the children up one behind the other, facing three objects placed in a straight line two metres apart. Each child has a turn at dribbling the ball in between and around the skittles. The game can be made into a competition, but it is not always necessary.

Hand-eye skills (9) (batting)

Bean bags, soft balls, and six bats are needed.

1. Pat a bean bag on the palm of the hand, making little taps upwards to project the bean bag into the air.
2. Throw the bean bag a little way upwards and catch it on the back of the hand.
3. Throw the bean bag into the air and try to hit it with the hand. Try to propel the bag forward.
4. Use soft balls of any size to practise batting the ball upwards. Try with the right hand, the left hand, both hands. Bat it, let it drop and catch it.
5. Toss the ball upwards, try to let the ball rebound on the head, let the ball drop and catch it.

Game. If there is a wall available, let the children practise batting their ball against a wall. Get them to count how many times they can bat the ball against the wall and let it bounce before it goes out of play. If there is limited wall space available arrange the class into stations:

Station 1. Batting the ball against the wall.
Station 2. Batting a bean bag over a bench to a partner.
Station 3. Two people hold hoops at head height. The others practise batting a bean bag through the hoop.
Station 4. Practising batting a large ball upwards with the flat of one hand, counting the number of times this can be done before the ball drops.
Station 5. With a partner. One child holds a bat at arm's length, the other throws a bean bag to hit the bat.

Foot-eye skills (3) outdoors — kicking

A large ball per child and six skittles are needed.

1. Putting the right foot on top of the ball and rolling the ball in the space near to the other foot. Repeat with the left foot.
2. Putting the balls on the ground and running around the balls between the spaces without touching the balls. When the teacher signals, running and putting one foot on top of own ball.
3. Line the children up facing one way. Practise kicking the ball forwards. On teacher's signal, the balls are collected.
4. Putting the ball on the ground and running and kicking the ball.
Teaching point — Encourage the children to keep their eyes on the ball as they kick it. Tell them to put their non-kicking foot alongside the ball and use the instep of the foot to kick the ball. Get them to try to make the instep face in the direction in which the ball is intended to travel.

Game. Arrange the class into stations.

Station 1. Practising kicking the ball at targets on a wall.
Station 2. Practising kicking the ball to hit an object such as a skittle, a box, or a tree.
Station 3. Practising kicking to score goals. Have one 'goal mouth' and a fielder to return the balls.
Station 4. Running and kicking for distance. 'How far?'

Hand-eye skills (10) — catching

One large ball per child is needed.

1. Drop the ball on the floor, let it bounce and catch it.
2. Walk around the area letting the ball drop, bounce and then catch it.

3. Toss the ball upwards with both hands and catch it.
4. If a wall is available, practise throwing the ball underarm at the wall and catching it before it bounces. The children should stand near the wall, about one stride away.
5. Hold the ball in both hands and run around the space. The teacher then says 'freeze', or 'jump on the spot', or 'stand on one leg', or 'crouch down', but the ball should not be dropped!

Game. This can be played indoors. Arrange the class into three circles. The first child in each circle gives the ball to the second, who bounces and catches the ball until the first child has run around the outside of the circle. When he is back in his place, the second child gives the ball to the third, and so on. The game can be played outdoors with a partner. The first child throws the ball to a partner who catches it and throws it back. The first child then holds the ball in both hands and runs around his partner. Take turns.

Activities with hoops

One hoop is needed for each child.

1. Put the hoop over the head, thread down the body and step out.
2. Put the hoop on the floor, step into it, thread the hoop along the body and lift it over the head.
3. Put the hoop on the floor. Run quickly in the spaces around the hoops, run anywhere in the area and on the teacher's directive return to the hoop.
4. Practise bowling the hoop along the ground.
5. Try to spin the hoop on the ground.
6. Try to hoola-hoop, spinning the hoop around the waist and hips and keeping one foot in front of the other.

Game

Take away four of the hoops. The children run quickly anywhere in the area, but do not touch the hoops or step inside them. On the teacher's signal, the children try to stand inside a hoop, one child in each hoop. Children without a hoop are 'losers'.

MIDDLE INFANTS

EVALUATION SHEET

	Co-operative	Listens to instructions	Accepted by peers	Leader?	Aiming	Dribbling	Kicking	Under-arm throw	Catching	
Name:										Teacher's comments
	✔	✔	✔	✔	✔	✔	✔	✔	X	

TOP INFANTS

Consult the evaluation sheet from the previous year's work. It should show clearly where there are any skill weaknesses. Start the year with one or two lessons (preferably outdoors), based on locomotor activities, and games without apparatus.

LOCOMOTOR SKILLS

Repeat the walking, running and jumping activities listed for the previous year and then add:

Walking

1. Long strides moving forwards.
2. Keep one foot still, make large lunges with the other foot in all directions, returning after each lunge to the start position. Change feet.
3. Walk as quickly as possible, forwards and backwards.
4. Walk on tiptoes, then normally, then walk with the body lowered and then walk with it raised again.
5. Walk so that one foot always stays behind the other. (The toes

of the back foot almost touch the heel of the front foot.)

6. Clap the hands in front and behind the body when walking.
7. Clap the hands under one leg when walking.
8. Walk in a circle clockwise then anticlockwise.

Running

1. Jog on the spot, then forwards, then run.
2. Run and after a signal, slow down, turn around and run in a new direction.
3. Run lifting the knees high, slap the knees as they come up.
4. Run with long bounding steps. Make a zig-zag pathway.
5. Run and on the teacher's signal, bend down, touch the ground and continue running.
6. Face one way and still maintaining that position, run and make a square pattern on the ground.
7. Face one way, run to the right, crossing the feet for four steps, then run to the left for four steps.

Jumping

1. Run, jump in the air and land to face a new way.
2. How far is it possible to travel forward with three jumps?
3. Jump with both feet together all over the area.
4. Jump in the air, landing in different ways with the feet in different positions — crossed, or one in front of the other, or on one foot, or wide apart. Experiment!
5. Run, jump high in the air and reach high with both hands.
6. As for point 5, but clap the hands.
7. Run, jump high in the air, with the arms by the sides of the body.

Games

These include games that have been mentioned previously — 'Grandmother's footsteps', 'Tom Tiddler's ground', and 'Lumps'.

'Busy Bee'. The class is divided into two equal groups. One group make a circle, drop their hands and stand still facing the centre of the circle. The children in the other group each find a partner. They stand facing one another, one step away and with their backs to the

centre of the circle. The teacher, or an extra child, stands in the centre of the circle and calls out various directions such as 'shake hands', 'touch noses', 'stand back to back', 'hop on the spot', etc. When she shouts 'Busy Bee', the outside circle of children find a new partner. The teacher also finds a partner. The child left without a partner is the new 'Busy Bee'.

'Crows and Cranes'. The class is divided into two groups 'Crows' and 'Cranes' which line up and face each other across a 5 metre space. The teacher calls Crrrrr . . . If 'Crows' is called, the 'Crows' chase the 'Cranes' to their line. If a 'Crane' is touched before he is safely over the line, he must join the 'Crows'. The group with the most players at the end of the time is the winner.

'Frost and Sun'. In the first stage, the teacher chooses three or four catchers, depending on the number of children. Any child touched by a catcher must stand still with his legs wide apart. The last four children to be touched are the new catchers. In the second stage of the game, any child who is not yet caught can 'un-freeze' a child who is standing still by crawling beneath the 'frozen' child's legs. The last four to be caught are the new catchers.

'Tail-tag'. All the children tuck a braid into the back of their waist bands to make a tail. Each child tries to catch as many 'tails' as she can.

MANIPULATIVE SKILLS

Bean bag activities

One bean bag per child is needed. Get them to:

1. Toss the bag upwards and catch it first with both hands, then with the right hand, then with the left hand.
2. Toss the bag upwards and 'catch' it on different parts of the body such as the back, head or back of the hands.
3. Toss the bean bag with the right hand, catch it with the left and vice versa.
4. Throw the bag upwards as high as possible and try to catch it.
5. Throw the bag upwards and clap the hands before catching the bag.

6. Try and throw the bag into the air from under the leg.
7. Throw the bean bag for distance, underarm (outdoors).
8. Practise batting the bean bag with the hand.

Game: 'Keep the basket full'

The teacher scatters the bean bags and the children try to return the bags to the teacher's basket. If the basket is empty, the teacher wins and if the basket is full, the children win.

Small ball activities

Hand-eye skills (11) (aiming)

A small ball is needed per child.

1. Throw the ball upwards and catch it with both hands.
2. Use the lines on the playground to roll the ball along.
   Teaching Point: remind the children to roll the ball smoothly by swinging the arm forward smoothly, bending the knees and stepping on the front foot as the ball is released.
3. With a partner about 5 paces apart, the sender aims at her partner who is crouched down, watching the ball, hands cupped and fingers pointing towards the ground. The receiver must be ready to move her feet to meet the oncoming ball.
4. With a partner: put two bean bags (or other markers) an equal distance from each player. The markers should be one child's step apart. Continue practising activity 3.

Game. Give six children a braid and a small ball. The rest of the children jump about the area with the feet together. The children with the balls roll them. If a ball touches a 'jumper' the jumper must stand still with legs astride.

Foot-eye skills (4) (outdoors) — dribbling, kicking and trapping

A large ball per child and eight skittles are needed.

1. Dribble the ball anywhere.
2. Dribble the ball and on a signal, kick it. After a second signal, chase after it and keep it still with one foot.
3. Put the right foot on top of the ball, use the foot to roll the ball near to and around the left foot and vice versa.

4.	Leave the balls on the ground. Run in and out of the spaces between them.

5.	Go back to your own ball. Take five steps away from the ball. Run and kick the ball. Take many turns and do not wait for a signal.

6.	With a partner, stand eight paces apart. Practise kicking and trapping the ball. Use 'Charlie Chaplin' feet to trap the ball, i.e. with the heels touching and the feet spread wide.

7.	Experiment. Push the ball with the outside of the foot and kick the ball with the inside of the foot.

Teaching point: the side of the foot should 'face' the receiver.

Game. The class is divided into stations.

Station 1:	Practise kicking the ball against the wall and trapping it on its return.

Station 2:	Three skittles (or three children) are placed in a line, 1 metre apart (or 2 paces). Take turns to dribble the ball in and out of the spaces.

Station 3:	Two markers for goal posts are placed eight paces apart. One goalkeeper is selected. Practise shooting goals.

Station 4:	Dribble the ball to a line, kick it and try to hit a skittle (or a box or a marker).

Station 5:	In twos, practise kicking and trapping the ball — choose the distance.

Large ball activities

Hand-eye skills (12) bouncing and rebounding

One large ball per child, three skittles, a bench, two ropes or some chalk and three hoops are needed.

1.	Drop the ball and catch it, first standing still, then walking around the area.

2.	Throw the ball upwards, let it bounce and then catch it.

3.	Throw the ball upwards, let it bounce, then use the fingers to bounce the ball down on the ground again and then catch it.

4.	Try to pat-bounce the ball twice, three times, or many times. Keep count.

5.	With a partner: put a hoop between two children. The children should face each other and be two paces away from the hoop. Practise bouncing the ball into the hoop. The partner should be ready to catch it or collect it.

Teaching Point: put two hands on top and slightly behind the ball, the backs of the hands 'facing' the thrower's body. Step onto one foot as you throw, push the ball downwards and look at the middle of the hoop.

Game. The class is divided into stations.

Station 1: Three skittles are placed in a line. Bounce and catch or pat-bounce the ball around the skittles.

Station 2: Use hoops instead of skittles and walk alongside them, bouncing the ball in each hoop and catching it.

Station 3: Place two skipping ropes or draw two lines with chalk 1 metre apart. Practise bouncing and catching or pat-bouncing between the lines.

Station 4: Drop and catch the ball as you walk along a bench.

Station 5: With a partner: one child holds a hoop at knee height, the other practises bouncing the ball into the hoop and catching it.

Large ball activities

Hand-eye skills (13) (throwing and catching)

One large ball is needed per child.

1. Toss the ball upwards and catch it.
2. Throw the ball upwards as high and as straight as possible, move the feet so that the body is under the ball, reach high with the hands and pull the ball into the body.
3. With a partner: stand two metres away. Practise throwing and catching the ball.

Teaching Point: remind the children to aim at their partner's chest, to step on the front foot and to bend their knee as they swing their arm forward. Remind the receivers to move into the line of the throw, to reach out with their hands, palms facing the oncoming ball, ready to close around the ball, their arms ready to bend and bring the ball into the chest.

Game. Circular passing rounders (see p. 106).

Small ball activities

Hand-eye skills (14) (throwing and catching)

One small ball is needed per child.
Repeat all the activities from the previous section using a small ball.

Hand-eye skills (15) (batting)

Each child needs a small ball and a bat.

1. Practise tossing the ball in the air and catching it.
   Experiment: Let it drop and catch it. Put it on the head and catch it as it falls. Throw or toss it in different ways with different hands.
2. Drop the ball and catch it. Pat-bounce the ball with one hand and then the other. Keep count.
3. Bat the ball forwards with one hand.
4. Use a bat preferably with a short handle and a large surface. Hold the bat in a chopper grip and practise turning the wrist so that each surface of the bat faces the ceiling or sky in turn. Do not change the grip.
5. Practise a chopping action. Bend and straighten the elbow and let the side of the bat 'chop' the air.
6. Hold the bat at arm's length, then to the right, across the body to the left, high in the air and low down.
7. Starting at a high point, trace a semi-circle with a sweeping arc until the bat is below the knee. (Make allowances for left- and right-handed players.)
8. Trace letters in the air. Spell out your name. Hold the bat firmly.
9. Run anywhere holding the bat in one hand. Keep the arm bent and tucked into the side.
10. As for point 9, but change direction on a signal.
11. Jump on the spot. Hold the bat firmly and keep the arm holding the bat bent. Rest the other hand on the surface of the bat.
12. Face the teacher. Skip-step to the right and skip-step to the left, holding the bat firmly.
13. Place a ball on the surface of the bat and hold it still.
14. Repeat point 13, but attempt to walk around the area.
15. Try and pat the ball upward a little way. See how many pats can be made before the ball drops to the ground.

Game. With a partner:

1. One child stands holding the bat at arm's length, the other stands five paces away, bowls underarm and tries to hit the bat.
2. When the ball hits the bat, the child holding the bat tries to push the ball back to the bowler.

Free practice

Allow the children to have a free choice of apparatus to practise with, such as large balls, small balls, bats, hoops, bean bags and skipping ropes.
Stations with selections of apparatus are suggested as follows:

Station 1: Foot-eye skill. Dribble, kick and shoot at goal.
Station 2: Pat-bouncing around skittles with a small ball.
Station 3: Free practice with a bat and a small ball.
Station 4: Throwing and catching in twos with a large ball.
Station 5: Practise aiming at different targets with a small ball — into a basket, at a skittle or into a hoop.
Station 6: Skipping.

There are other games that some top infants can play. These are listed below:

French cricket

Five cricket bat shapes and five balls are needed.
Divide the class into five groups. One child holds the bat and tries to protect his legs. The other children aim the ball at the batsman's legs, the batsman bats the ball away. If a child is successful in aiming and touches the batsman's leg, this child becomes the new batsman.

'Skittle ball'

The class is divided into two teams, red and blue. A blue skittle is placed inside a blue hoop about twelve metres opposite and away from a red skittle in a red hoop. The blue team try to knock down the red skittle and vice versa. The teacher and the children can make their own rules!

'Shoot-ball'

Divide the class into two teams. Suspend two hoops at the height of the teacher's outstretched arm or borrow the junior netball posts. Try to provide as many balls as possible. Each child shoots at goal. One child collects all the balls that have passed through the ring and puts them in a basket. The teacher gives the stop signal. All the class count the balls in the baskets. They call one 'one', 'two', 'three' etc.

'Back to back'

There must be an uneven number of players. The teacher calls out 'hop around the room' and then 'backs' at which, the children must stand back to back and link arms. The child who is left alone is the loser. The game starts again with 'skip anywhere' and then 'backs', etc. A variation could be to find a partner and shake hands.

'Mouse-trap'

Half the class hold hands in a circle and these children lift their arms high to form arches. The rest of the class are the 'mice' and can skip in and out of the circle through the arches. When the teacher calls 'trap', the circle of children bring their arms down to try to catch the mice. Mice who are caught join the trappers.

'Pass the parcels'

The children sit or stand in a circle. Objects are then passed around the circle. Start by giving a bean bag to the first, tenth and twentieth child and then as the passing continues, give a ball to the second, eleventh and twenty first child, etc. The idea is to try to catch a child with two objects!

'Straddle ball'

The class make a circle. Each child stands with his/her legs astride so that his/her feet touch the next person's feet. Four children are placed in the centre of the circle and each are given a ball. On the teacher's signal, the four children can move where they like, on the next signal, they roll their balls to try to get them through the legs of one of the children in the circle. If they are successful, they change places. If not, they stay in the centre!

'London Bridge'

Ten children make arches by holding both of their hands high (like London Bridge). The other children run or walk through the arches.

If the teacher says 'down!' any child trapped under the falling arches is caught. As soon as two people are caught, they form a new arch.

EQUIPMENT

Ideally, there should be enough small apparatus for each child to have one item each from the following list:

Bean bags: 32-8 in each of the following colours, red, green, blue and yellow.
Large balls: 30 size 5 made of plastic-coated sponge rubber or of coloured plastic (red, green, yellow, blue).
Small balls: 30 foam or sponge balls or tennis balls.
Bat shapes: 30 with short handles and a wide batting surface.
Braids: 32-8 each of the following colours (red, green, blue, yellow).
Hoops: 30 in plastic in four colours (red, green, yellow and blue). Perhaps 15 with a diameter of 60 cm and 15 with a diameter of 92 cm.

Other useful items

Skittles — adjustable plastic in four colours. (*Cones* might be easier to store because they stack so easily.)
Baskets made of plastic coated wire to use both as containers and obstacles.
Playground chalk, a block measuring 50 mm in by 30 mm.
A whistle.
Skipping ropes of various lengths — 2 metres and 3 metres.
Nets (3) to store the large balls.
Cricket bat shapes (5).
Plastic balls shaped like rugby balls (5).

USEFUL BOOKS

A. Cooper, *The Development of Games Skills* (Basil Blackwell, Oxford, 1982).

P. Wetton, *Bright Ideas, Games for Physical Education* (Scholastic Publications, 1987).

TOP INFANTS

EVALUATION SHEET

Name:	Co-operative	Listens to instructions	Accepted by peers	Leader?	Learning to accept rules	Aiming	Dribbling	Kicking	Trapping	Underarm throw	Catch large ball	Pat-bounce	Batting	Teacher's comments
	✔	✔				✔		✔		✔	✔	✔		

7

Dance in the Infant School

Creative and rhythmic dance is a very important element in children's lives which we cannot ignore. Children love to move rhythmically and are always delighted to be allowed to express themselves openly in response to sounds, words and music.

Dance is a medium which can be used to help children's aesthetic development. It gives the children a chance 'to feel' a rhythm or a mood, as they move to a piece of music, or a poem, or a beat of the drum. It is also a vehicle through which children can come to understand the moods and rhythms of other cultures when teachers select say, Indian, or African dance music.

Dance takes many forms in infant schools and children can be exposed to creative dance, folk or country dance, or movement associated with the theme being explored in the classroom.

Teachers, however, vary in their enthusiasm to teach dance and many thousands of teachers have been grateful for the support of the BBC in producing the two radio programmes 'Let's Move' and 'Time to Move', which are broadcast weekly during term time on Radio 4. These programmes provide 'a rich source of music, much of it specially commissioned and arranged specifically for young children's creative movement and dance'.[1] A theme is developed by the broadcasts in easy movement stages and follow-up activities are suggested. Here are a few suggestions on how BBC programmes might best be used.

Wherever possible, the programmes should be taped so that the class teacher can make an input to the lesson. In this way, the programmes can be used as a support and stimulus through which children are encouraged to express themselves, whilst the teacher is involved, as always, in the very important task of observation. The tape can be stopped when the teacher feels that the quality of the children's movement could be improved by a useful teaching point, or a demonstration, or by giving extra help to individuals. For example, 'If you all tuck your heads in and curl your bodies we can make a much clearer small shape,' or 'John, would you like to show us your slithery snake? Watch the way he curves and twists his spine.' If the teacher does not make an input, there is the likelihood that the broadcasts will become dull rather than exciting. Since the broadcaster is not in contact with the children, she cannot observe their reactions to stimuli and cannot therefore develop the children's responses. Also, the BBC programme will not necessarily 'match' the theme being explored in the classroom and may take up valuable time which could be used to better effect.

There is no doubt that when individual teachers create, teach and develop their own materials, there is a much better result. Many infant school teachers and student teachers have become very confident and successful at this skill, I think, because they value the opportunity to reinforce and extend the work which they are exploring in the classroom. Classroom teachers are also more aware of the links which can be made because they are more conversant with their own children and with the curriculum as a whole, particularly with regard to language and mathematics, than is the BBC presenter. It may seem perhaps, rather odd to be talking about language development in a discussion concerning the importance of dance, but it has been suggested that a long-term objective in school should be to develop language across the curriculum (Bullock Report).[2] However, physical education can and does play an important part in this total development. Physical educationists have always known that children can learn new language during PE lessons and can also repeat and practise language already assimilated. A closer examination of our work, however, would reveal the very special language to which a child is exposed during such lessons. The primary object in physical education is not to develop language skills *per se*, but if we are to accept that we are responsible for educating the 'whole child', then we must be aware of the learning potential within the physical education environment, particularly if the programme is structured to correspond to the theme being explored in the classroom. Language is not taught; it is acquired with usage and lessons in physical education offer a stimulating environment with wide opportunities for language development. Verbal interactions during physical activity between teacher and child and child and peer, offer an area of language not necessarily explored elsewhere. The child, especially one for whom English is a second language, can talk about action concepts expressed by such verbs as 'touch', 'run', 'jump' and 'walk' and can experience the action physically at the same time. The teacher can talk to the children about spatial concepts and directional concepts whilst the children are physically involved in carrying out the action. Such words as 'in front of', or 'behind' may not have meant much in the classroom, but now begin to make sense. With this increase in understanding and range of vocabulary, the children may also develop an ability to verbalise their own feelings. A reticent child, who makes no contribution to classroom discussion or who is unable to write down his thoughts, may find the task of expressing his enjoyable experience in physical education lessons in written work somewhat easier.[3]

Language can also play an important part in helping children to develop quality in movements. Some of this language will be fundamental, for example, action words such as run, skip, walk, jump, hop, slide, (locomotor) and twist, turn, bend, stretch, swing, (non-locomotor). Some of the language will be expressive — stamp, march, slither, scurry, etc. (locomotor) and reach, crouch, screw, explode, etc. (non-locomotor). There is also more elaborate language — locomotor — crawl and creep very smoothly, whirl and swirl round quickly like a tornado and non-locomotor — twist slowly, push, push your knees, etc. These are just some examples of the language that is available to us to stimulate and give quality to the children's movements.

In addition, the teacher can also add to the quality of the movements by using her voice in different ways. For instance, there is more possibility of eliciting a good movement response if the teacher chooses her words carefully and emphasises certain syllables or introductory sounds — 'The softly, bending swaying willow', (quiet, soft tones, prolonged delivery) 'was suddenly bit*te*n with the *c*old, *c*risp, fro*st*' (quick, sharp tones with the emphasis on the sharp-sounding letters). A good movement response at any age can also be enhanced by the teacher if she can involve her class in moving to a catchy verse which the pupils can verbalise as they move. There are many action rhymes that can be used and teachers often make up their own. No one should doubt the linguistic value of chanting words as actions are performed. If the words can then be written in a child or teacher-made book, the true value will be noted as the children 'read' or read the book. For example,

I can jump, jump, jump,
I can hop, hop, hop,
Watch me, watch me,

See me flop!
I can skip, skip, skip,
I can trot, trot, trot,
Watch me, watch me,
See me flop!

There are many body action chants that can be created by either the teacher or the children. These are extensions of the finger-play rhymes used in the classroom. For example,

Susan is a window cleaner,
Swish, swish, swish,
She likes to clean the windows,
Swish, swish, swish.

She likes to climb the ladder,
Step, step, step,
Down again, down again,
Step, step, step,

or

I can be a joiner,
Knocking in the nails,
Get them out of boxes,
Get them out of pails.

Knock them in the ceiling,
Knock them in the ground,
Hammer, hammer, hammer,
Hammer all around.

With these rhymes, it is always best to let the children themselves decide which actions should be used and to encourage them to use their whole bodies.

. Young entrants to the reception class will probably also enjoy moving to some of the well-known nursery rhymes. The children can begin to express themselves through body actions to a known rhyme and also begin to feel the rhythm of the verse. It is a good idea to say the rhymes in the classroom first and perhaps clap the hands or tap a foot whilst saying the words before moving into larger actions, particularly as many of the younger children cannot yet skip or trot or march to a given beat. For example, the rhyme

One, two, buckle my shoe,
Three, four, knock at the door,
Five, six, pick up sticks,
Seven, eight, lay them straight,
Nine, ten a big fat hen

shows too how children can reinforce their number sense as they build up rhyme rhythms and use body actions. There are many opportunities for children to learn mathematical concepts and to practise, reinforce and learn mathematical language whilst they are happily involved in dance activities. Teachers should be constantly aware of the mathematical possibilities that present themselves.

BODY SHAPE

Teachers encourage children to be aware of shape and size very early on in infant school and in fact, it is a constant and necessary theme which is explored in number, language, art and craft and most areas of the curriculum. Body shape is also a constant and underlying theme in expressive movement. It is logical, therefore, when exploring the theme of shape in the classroom to also explore the same theme in physical education lessons. A good way to start with reception class children is, as stated previously, to use action songs and rhymes. One very well-known rhyme that is particularly useful at this stage is:

Example One: 'The crooked man' (irregular shape)

Practise 'crooked' movements and carry them out to the sound of castanets or drum.

1. Bend the fingers at both joints, first the left hand, then the right.
2. Twist the hands: bend the wrists backwards, forwards, inwards, outwards to sharp quick movements on castanets — 'clack'. Hold until the next movement.
3. Bend the elbow. On each 'clack' of the castanet, move the elbow sharply to a new place — out, up, down.
4. Put the head in different positions — (castanet).

5. Bend knees and ankles — make angular shapes. (castanet).
6. Walk around to the right, then the left and bang the knees — to the sound of a drum.
7. Walk with one foot turned out and the other turned in, again to a drum beat.
8. Stand on the spot. *Experiment.* Stick one hip out, one knee out. Each time the drum beats, the children can choose a part of the body to stick out.

Other ideas on exploring shape and size include:

Example two: wide, tall, small (regular shape and size)

Practise growing, shrinking and moving in these shapes to the sound of a tambourine.

1. Start in a small curled shape, grow slowly and smoothly until the body is tall and stretched high. (The tambourine gently rattles until all the children are stretched tall and standing still).
2. Use the same sound to move the children from tall to small, small to wide, wide to tall, etc.
3. Use a drum and on each loud beat, ask the children to change their shape and size. Encourage them to hold the shape for a few moments, ready to change.
4. Practise walking around the area in each of the different shapes and sizes. (Change the drum beat for each one.)

Divide the class into three groups and make a pattern/dance, for example, tall people walk into the middle until their shoulders touch, wide people walk into the centre and make a circle, hands touching and surround the tall people. Small people scurry under the wide people's legs, turn round and come out again.
Another shape activity is to use circles as a theme.

Example three: circles (regular shape)

Use the record Ravel's *Bolero*.

1. Practise drawing circles in the air with one finger — small circles (50 cm in diameter) using finger joints to create the circle.

2. Draw circles with the ends of all the fingers, the movement is around the wrist.
3. Draw circles with the movement starting from shoulder. Use the whole arm and stretch the fingertips to make a big circle.
4. Use one finger, or use two fingers together to make two circles, or use both wrists.
5. Use both arms and stand with the arms stretched, palms touching and let each arm move outwards as far as possible then downwards to meet each other.

Dance

Any folk dance record can be used.

1. Each child puts a hoop on the ground and skips round it.
2. Form the class into a circle with the hands joined.
3. Skip around in the circle and stop.
4. Drop hands, turn and face the back of the person in front and skip in a circle.
5. Join hands, skip into the circle and out again.

Example four: 'Once upon a time . . . '

'Goldilocks . . . walked along a straight pathway; she walked past some tall thin trees; she walked past some crooked, spikey trees; then she saw some small, curved bushes. She continued to walk, but the pathway started to wind about curving from one place to another. She came to a very low bridge over the path and she had to either curl up small to go under it or make a very wide step to step over it.

It was getting colder now so she decided to run, she ran on a straight path, then the path started to twist and turn until suddenly she saw a house. It had a square door. And round circles for windows. And tall, thin chimney pots.

And a peculiar shaped door knocker which was very high up on the door. She stretched her arm high, very high, she stood on tiptoes, but she could not reach it. What could she do?' (Ask the children.) 'Suddenly the door opened. She saw, a great big, wide grandfather clock and it went: tick — tock, tick — tock.' (Use one arm to make a sweeping half circle up and down.) She saw: a middle-sized ordinary grandmother clock and it went: tick, tock, tick, tock, tick, tock, tick, tock.' (Bend one arm and lift one hand to the shoulder and down again.) 'And then she saw a little, small weeny baby clock and it went: tick, tick, tick, tick, tick, tick, tick.' (Use one wrist to move the hand up and down as quickly as possible.)

Continue the story and develop the movements as appropriate. The story can end with the children either running away or quietly lying down to go to sleep. A good way of continuing this activity after the lesson would be to encourage the children to make their own 'shape' story book in the classroom.

There are many other movement themes which match the class work in which children are involved. Some suggestions, together with ways of developing them are as follows — 'Ourselves' or 'My body', 'People who help us', 'Toys', 'Spring', 'Animals', 'Transport', 'Time', 'Machines', 'Water', 'Winter' and 'The Circus'. Festivals such as Bonfire Night or Halloween are also suitable themes.

OURSELVES OR MY BODY

Introduction

Play a record or tape with a definite beat — marching music such as *Stars and Stripes* (Sousa) M1 or the *Radetzky March* (Strauss).

1. Walk around the area to the music.
2. Walk and swing the arms high.
3. Walk and lift the knees high.

Movement training

1. *'Heads and Shoulders, Knees and Toes'*.M2
2. Fingers. Explore all possible finger movements — single finger, similar finger on eac: hand, all the fingers. Practise meeting and parting fingers — ப⸴ ⸳h, low. Practise moving fingers in and out of each other.
3. Tap the fingers together, clap the hands, form fists.
4. Hands: Stretch and curl the hands.
5. Arms: Move the wrists, elbows, shoulders in and out, up and down, circling, shaking, making pathways. Use one arm,

both arms together or arms intertwining.

6. Legs: Hips, knees, ankles can be moved as follows. Clap the knees, swing one leg and pivot on the heel to turn the ankle out.

7. Feet: Toes, heels and sides of feet — explore the possibilities for movement.
   Walk on toes, sit down and clap the feet.
   Walk with the feet together and apart.
   Walk with the heels together and the feet turned out.

8. Try combining some of the movements — Walk with toes turned in whilst circling the wrists.
   Sit down and clap the hands and feet.

Dance ideas

1. Have a conversation with a partner using hand movements.
2. Walk alone or with a partner. Find different ways of meeting and parting with different parts of the body.

Locomotion with emphasis on the feet

A drum can be used for these movements.

Introduction

1. Walk anywhere.
2. Walk and stop.

Movement training

1. Walk on tiptoes, or the heels, or the outside or insides of the feet.
2. Skip, hop, run, jump — encourage the children to change direction. Observe and comment on the way the children use their feet.
3. Skip, hop, run, jump — practise stopping and starting.
4. Practise accelerating and decelerating.
5. Move near to the ground — walking, running or jumping?

Dance ideas

1. With a partner, try walking together, try different formations — side by side, one in front of the other.
2. Make a foot pattern when dancing alone.

3. With a partner, one leads the other follows. Use the feet in different ways.

Using different body parts with emphasis on the trunk

A drum and a tambourine can be used.

Introduction

1. Run anywhere.
2. Run lifting the knees high.

Movement training

1. Bend at the waist, flop over.
2. Bend at the waist, lean backwards.
3. Twist the upper body, keeping the feet still.
4. Swing the hips from side to side.
5. Lift one hip and move it round and round in a circle.
6. Stick the tummies, seats and chests out!

Dance ideas

1. What part of the body begins with the letter T? Stick it out and walk around! (Repeat with other parts of the body.)
2. Make a floppy shape. Shake all over with every part of the body. Flop forwards, leave the arms swinging and move about the room.

Try to encourage the children to be more aware of the different parts of their bodies when they go back into the classroom. Let them draw or paint a picture of themselves. See if the detail improves after each dance lesson.

PEOPLE WHO HELP US

These include the fireman, nurse, painter, soldier, builder, policewoman, etc. When visitors come to the school to explain the work that they do, children enjoy the chance to pretend that they are that person doing that job. In the classroom, teachers will probably set up the 'home corner' so that the children can role play and make believe that they are, for example, in the fire station. In dance, another dimension can be added, that of gross motor and locomotor practice.

Fireman

Introduction

Use a bell and let the children pretend they are driving the fire engine. (If there are enough quoits available, use them as steering wheels.)

Movement training

1. Practise climbing up the ladder. Reach high, lift the knees high.
2. Pretend to lift an object from the floor.
3. Push an imaginary object.
4. Pull an imaginary object.
5. What would it be like to move on a floor which was very hot?
6. What would it be like to move about where parts of the walls and the furniture had fallen down?
7. Practise winding up a long hose into a circle.

Dance ideas

1. A hot floor dance on an imaginary hot floor — sharp, quick movements.
2. A story about fire.

Use tone blocks, tulip blocks and castanets to produce sharp sounds. Let the children make hissing and sizzling sounds to give an atmosphere of heat.

TOYS

This theme can be explored around Christmas time. Children like to pretend they are toys, which come to life at midnight as the clock strikes twelve!

Marionettes[M3] or 'Puppet on a string'. Sandie Shaw.

1. With a partner, one child pretending to be the puppet. Face 'the marionette' . . . pull imaginary strings. Pretend to pull an elbow string . . . put the pulling hand near to the elbow, do not touch it . . . as you pull, the elbow moves in that direction. Try the elbows, hands, knees, toes and head.
2. Let one child sit on the floor and let the other pull the strings . . . perhaps two together?

147

3. Practise jiggling parts of the body.

4. Now practise being a marionette on your own. Practise moving parts of the body . . . look where the string would be . . . move slowly, let the parts flop back again.

5. Practise walking . . . slow, wobbly steps, knees bending out and in, arms flopping.

6. Practise moving the head from side to side and up and down with a jerk.

Mechanical toys

The *Nutcracker Suite* by Tchaikovsky[M4] could be played.

Musical-box fairies

1. Smooth, 'beautiful' movements on the spot.
2. Make a beautiful shape. Practise turning one way and then the other.
3. Practise arm movements and make a repeatable pattern, e.g. three different arm movements then a turn of the body, a movement of the head — repeat.

Robots

1. Wind the robots up. Let the children make a sound to tell us that the key is turning. Let them wind up an imaginary toy. (Quick turning movements of the wrist.)

2. Practise movements with straight limbs.

3. Sit with a straight back and the legs straight out and practise turning the head with a jerky movement. Practise arm movements, bending at the elbow.

4. Let the children create a mechanical dance that can be repeated over and over.

Bendy doll[M5]

1. Practise 'bendy' movements — at the waist.
2. Make a curved shape? Make a curved bend around the elbow. Curl the arms around the body, around the neck.
3. Sit down and place the legs in strange places — around the neck? Wrap one leg around the other?
4. Tie yourself into a bendy knot.
5. Make slow, smooth movements.

Train^{M6}

1. Find a partner. Practise walking one behind the other without touching each other.
2. Hold the partner's waist and practise walking together, slowing down and stopping.
3. As for 1 and 2, but with four people.

Spanish doll^{M7}

1. Walk with a straight back, head looking over one shoulder.
2. Practise making shapes with the arms — one high in the air, one across the body.
3. Step on one foot and pivot on the heel of the other.
4. Practise tapping first one heel, then the other.
5. Practise turning and pivoting on the spot with one arm held high and the other behind the back.

Give the children the chance to work together and have the experience of moving in the 'character' of each make-believe toy, then let them choose which they would like to be. Sometimes children ask to be a different kind of toy! You will need to be inventive if this happens.

SPRING — PLANTS

Introduction

Any lively activity such as jumping or hopping. Use wood blocks to make a rhythmic beating sound or a drum, tambourine, etc.

Movement training

Ideas include growing . . . plants, shape . . . trees. Talk quietly about growing and uncurling smoothly.

1. Sit and uncurl one finger from a clenched fist.
2. Now uncurl two fingers together.
3. Now uncurl five fingers, one at a time, one, two, three, four, five — first, second, third, fourth, fifth.

4. Repeat with two hands together.
5. Curl up close to the ground but stay on the feet. Grow upwards, uncurling until stretched high. Return to start.
6. Trees — 'What shape do trees grow into?' — apple, poplar, beech. oak, holly, hawthorn, etc. Talk about the different shapes, practise making the different shapes — are they symmetrical or asymmetrical? Let the children choose . . . start close to the ground and grow into a different tree shape each time.
7. 'What other things grow from the soil in spring?' e.g. strawberry suckers . . . along the ground. Practise moving on fronts, on backs, 'growing' along the floor smoothly. Also, beans . . . tendrils . . . twisting and curling as they grow in height.

Dance ideas

1. Growing into different shapes from different positions.
2. With two people, one grows upwards, the other outwards — then change places. Keep returning to a low position.

SPRING — ANIMALS

Ideas include growing . . . frogs — use a tambourine or voice sounds.

Introduction

Hopping and leaping movements.

Movement training

1. 'Jelly on the plate,
   Jelly on the plate,
   Wibble, wobble,
   Wibble, wobble,
   Jelly on the plate.'
2. Frogspawn inside the jelly — wobble. (Accompany with a tambourine.)

3. Try wobbling whilst lying down. (Accompany with a tambourine.)
4. Lie down — curl up — slowly stretch both legs out together — a tadpole. (Scratch on a tambourine.)
5. Try and move along the ground without using arms or feet — a tadpole. (Accompany with a tambourine.)
6. Grow frog's leg one at a time — talk about the shape, the angles . . .
7. Curl up — grow legs — stand on four legs . . . frog jumping about the room . . .

Progression

Use the description of Hens — eggs and chickens from the story: *The Speckled Hen* by Alison Uttley[4] (p. 7) and also *The Little Red Hen* (p. 37).[5] To imitate a hen, place the legs wide apart — legs bent, tummies and chests out, arms bent, elbows pointing backwards. Practise strutting, practise head movements, wiggle the tail feathers and practise pecking with sharp, sudden movements.

THE CIRCUS[M7]

This theme can become a school theme and could be used to celebrate the end of a school year which culminates in a school circus that parents could also become involved in. The circus provides us with a community of characters, an abundance of colour, shape, design and technology, which can be explored by the children both in the classroom and in movement.

Clowns

Practise different ways of walking. Toes turned in, toes turned out, wobbly legs, 'Charlie Chaplin feet, slow, deliberate long steps, walking slowly with the knees high. Practise pretending to 'trip'. Practise a fall. Remind the children about the size and shape of the clown's clothes — his shoes and his hat.

Acrobats

Teach the children a tumbling routine in their gymnastics lesson.

Hoola-Hoop

Practise with hoops in the games lesson.

Tightrope

Practise balancing activities in the gymnastics lesson. Use the balance side of a bench.

Band

1. Practise walking in time to the music of a marching band.
2. Practise pretending to play an instrument.
3. Combine points 1 and 2.
4. Practise walking with two people behind two, then four people behind four.

Jugglers

Practise ball skills in a games lesson.

Seals

Children move about on their hands, their tummies facing the floor and some of their weight resting on the lower leg as they drag their bodies around the area. Let them rest and clap their 'flippers'.

Horses

Practise stepping on the spot with knees high. Practise trotting, then 'dressage' trotting. Trot behind each other in a line moving around the circus ring. Hold the front 'legs' high on the chest. Invent patterns, depending on the children's ability.

Elephants

Walk heavily on flat feet, bend the back so that the head is bent forwards, use an arm to represent a trunk. Plod about the area, swinging the trunk. Pretend to put the trunk in a bucket of water, then pretend to spray the audience. The elephants can move in a line if the
spare arm is used as a tail.

Let the children choose which act they would like to be in after they
have practised all the activities. Choose a teacher to be ringmaster!

Children become very confident when they work with the teacher
on a class theme that is taken into the larger space such as the
hall. They are confident because they have already, in most cases,
listened to stories, painted pictures, become involved in functional
and make-believe play and, I think, have a base of knowledge from
which to develop their creative and expressive movement activities.
In the medium of creative movement, they can express themselves
in a non-competitive, unthreatening way at their own individual rate
of learning. We can excite them and challenge them too to add quality
to their movement as they seek the full physical range of movements
available to them. Teachers should try to keep a balance between
praising creative ideas that are executed in a superficial way and praising those who excel at perfected movements. Always expect more
from the children — 'I like that idea Mark — can you move your
head from side to side quickly? I think that will make you really look
like a hen.'

My suggestions are just starting points. Most of my student teachers
develop much more exciting and creative movement ideas when they
begin to work with their own children.

Another aspect of dance which we can usefully explore with infant
school children is rhythmic dance, sometimes called country dance
or folk dance. Most of the ideas suggested here can be developed in
many ways simply by varying the type of music used. For instance,
when playing musical games or singing songs, teachers can choose
music from France, Asia, India or the West Indies, as well as, or
instead of, British regional music. Much depends on the cultural
background of the children in the class and the kind of atmosphere
that the teacher wishes to create. The staff in the school will probably have decided together whether the children in Northumberland,
for example, should begin to understand only their own cultural tradi-
tions or whether, through dance, they can begin to experience the
'feel' of, say, Japanese culture, or Asian culture.

FOLK DANCE

There are many ways in which teachers can help younger children to start to enjoy folk dancing and many methods which can be used to lead children into dancing in formal formations, but central to them all, is a need for children to be able to step and move rhythmically to the beat of the music. Most of our young children, however, do not find this easy and we do not always introduce them to this aspect of dance in a helpful way. One common mistake we make is to thrust them into Maypole dancing, or into dancing for a parents evening without giving them any pre-dancing experience and without allowing them to develop their dancing skills slowly. There has to be a slow build-up of the skills needed for folk dancing if the activity is to be enjoyable. Children need to become good listeners. They need to be able to hear the changes in the music and to develop a more formalised approach to the notion of stepping for sixteen, eight, four or two steps and to the notion of specific dance steps and formations. There has to be an obvious link between the music and the movement born of good auditory skills. This can only be achieved with sensible planning. Children should have the opportunity to develop their folk-dancing skills year by year and some allowance for this should be made in the prepared syllabus.

There are many enjoyable methods of introducing children to folk dancing, and teachers, I am sure, will have already tried some of them before. One method is to play some of the musical games that are popular at children's parties, for example, 'Musical Mats', 'Musical Statues' or 'Musical Hoops'. Children can listen carefully for the time when the music stops. Continue this development by asking the children to join hands with a partner whilst playing the games. This helps the children to begin to co-ordinate their movements with another person. It also provides the necessary foundation for later dances.

Another method to use in the early stages is to play the clapping games which most of us experienced in our own childhood. Arrange the class in pairs and ask them to show you a clapping rhyme. Use one of the simpler combinations and encourage the rest of the class to make an exact reproduction of the rhythm.

Also, it is a good idea to introduce children to a collection of songs in their music lessons that they will eventually be able to sing and dance to. I received a good tip once from an experienced teacher who had had some very successful sessions of folk dancing. She had introduced her children to a collection of World War II songs and when the children were at the stage when they were overheard singing them in the playground and corridors, she used them to dance to.[M8]

A method I also use to stimulate rhythmic movement is to beat on a drum. The drum gives a clear, distinguishable sound that helps the children to respond without much difficulty. It does not create the same 'mood' as recorded music or singing familiar songs and sometimes tends to move into African-type movements. Nevertheless, the drumbeat does give the teacher and the children a chance to consider the different rhythms that people from other cultures can experience.

Whichever method you use, try to keep the lessons informal and happy occasions. In the early stages, try not to formalise the rhythms or movements into conformist patterns which often restrict the movements of young children. Try not to insist on keeping to set routines where children have to move for eight steps or four steps or have to remember long sequences. Infant school children are generally too young to cope with these kinds of concepts and as with any other subject, they need to be introduced to known dances gradually. The important task in the infant school is to lay a firm foundation so that the children can eventually progress to formalised dancing at a later stage.

A good way to progress from these suggested, simple openings is to concentrate on clapping rhythms or word rhythms, or voice rhythms.

Name rhythms and movements

1. Sit in a circle with shoulders touching and facing inwards.
2. Each person says their own name *in turn* three times.
3. Repeat but build. The teacher starts, the next child joins in, etc. until everybody is speaking.
4. Repeat point 2 above, but add an arm/hand movement.
5. Repeat point 3 above but add an arm/hand movement.
6. No sound . . . movement only. One starts, the next joins in until everybody is moving.
7. Stand up and repeat point 6.
8. Choose a leg movement. The teacher does her movement, the next child joins in and so on until everybody is moving.
9. Allow children to move around the room making no sound at all.
10. Ask the children to choose a soft sound to accompany their movement.

Voice rhythms and movements!

1. Sitting in a circle, think of a noise.
2. The teacher starts, the next child joins in, until everybody is making a sound. Stress the need for soft sounds, sharp sounds and 'variations'. Make sure you have a signal for *stop*.
3. The teacher makes a movement to fit her sound then proceeds as for point 2.
4. Everyone stands and chooses a movement to take them from the floor to above their own height. The teacher starts and everyone joins in as usual until the whole class is involved.
5. The teacher starts her movement, the next child may either copy her or choose his own movement and so on around the class. (Three or four may copy.
6. Widen the circle to use the whole room. Choose a name and use it to create a movement pattern to take each child into the centre of the room and out again.
7. Practise a sound which starts at a low pitch and increases to a high one.
8. Choose a movement to match the sound in point 7 .
9. Practise a sound which starts at a low pitch, moves to a high pitch and returns to a low pitch again.
10. Chose a movement to match the sound.
11. Shadow-punching *alone*.
12. Shadow-kicking *alone*.
The teacher decides if points 11 and 12 should be attempted in pairs!

Clapping rhythms and movement (I)

1. Sing and clap together:
'If you are happy and you know it,
Clap your hands.
If you are happy and you know it,
Clap your hands,
If you are happy and you know it,
And you really want to show it,
If you are happy and you know it,
Clap your hands.'
2. The children can continue to sing the song with the children, but can suggest that the children clap their hands in a different place

each time such as above their hands, behind their backs, high in the air, etc.

3. The teacher starts by clapping a rhythm, e.g. clap knees, clap hands, clap knees, clap hands. The children join in. Try a few more ideas — head and hands; shoulders and hands.

4. Walk anywhere and with the left foot down, clap hands, then with the right foot down, clap hands. Try walking forwards, try walking backwards.

5. Follow-my-leader. Form the class into one long line. Practise point 4 and get everyone to try and keep in line.

Dance idea

All the children stand in a straight line, one behind the other. The teacher tells them they are going to make a circle by following her. Use the walk and clap the rhythm when making the circle. Stand still. Clap the hands and knees and then the heads and hands for a few times. Clap the hands together and finish by singing and clapping to the song 'If you are happy and you know it'.

N.B. Challenge the children. If they cannot clap the rhythms, laugh about it! Ask them to ask their dads if they can do it!

Clapping rhythms and movement (II)

With a partner. Use a folk dance record.[M9]

Introduction

1. Skip around the room following a partner.
2. Skip around the room holding hands with a partner.

Movement training

1. Hold both hands across with a partner and skip around in a circle.
2. Put a hoop on the floor, follow your partner and skip around the hoop. Turn and go the other way when teacher says 'change'.
3. Face each other across the hoop. Both skip once around the hoop. Face your partner and shake right hands. Repeat.

Partner dance

1. Face your partner.
2. Clap right hands four times then left hands four times.

3. Clap both hands with your partner four times.
4. Clap your own hands four times.
5. Your partner stands still, clapping his hands whilst you walk/skip around him.
6. You clap whilst your partner skips around you.
7. Repeat.

Try and introduce some folk music to dance to, preferably from your own region. Try and choose some music where a folk song has been recorded so that the children can sing as they dance. This will create an atmosphere more redolent and typical of folk dancing and the children may find it easier to be more rhythmical in the more relaxed environment. Remember that folk dancing is a social activity and that keeping the flow of the dance is more important than the steps, particularly at an early stage. So do not worry if the children clap three times instead of four, or if they skip for nine steps instead of eight steps!

Remember too, to include music from other cultures if your school is in a multi-cultural area. Some of the other cultures have much more formalised dances and this may be a good time and a good opportunity to involve some of the parents in helping to create them.

Once the children can be observed to be able to walk and skip to folk-dance music they can be introduced to more formal formations. For example, suggest that the children walk for eight steps then stand on the spot and 'mark time' for eight steps. The teacher can direct at first and then see if the children can do the manoeuvre themselves. Try not to insist on walking and walking on the spot to rigid counting. Instead, give the children plenty of time to begin and finish one manoeuvre before starting another. Progress to holding hands with a partner and completing the same pattern of walking eight steps forward and eight steps on the spot. Then repeat this pattern, but this time walk backwards. Try repeating all three stages using a skipping step. Now combine the manoeuvres into a dance. Make the class form a circle and give alternate children a braid to wear. The children and the teacher walk briskly around the area with the hands joined (about sixteen steps). Everybody drops hands and walks on the spot (for about ten steps). Everybody wearing a braid walks into the middle of the circle for eight steps, then walks on the spot for eight steps and then walks backwards to the starting position in the circle. People not wearing braids can clap their hands whilst they wait for their turn. Then repeat.

Variations can be as follows:

1. Make circles of eight around the area and repeat the dance.
2. Use a skipping step throughout.
3. Make the class form a circle. At the point where the dancers move into the centre of the circle, let pairs of children hold hands and move in together.
4. Repeat point 3, but instead of holding hands, the children hold braids between them.

Progress to building up a repertoire of skills:

1. Long steps, small steps, skips, hops, jumps, using the heels, using the toes.
2. Work around obstacles such as skittles or hoops. Walk from a starting position around the obstacle and back to the start. Try going round one way and then the other. Try a 'do-si-do'. (Walk forwards, side step the obstacle and come back backwards.)
3. Introduce simple counting — Clap eight times, listen for eight, nod the head four times, listen for four, shrug the shoulders four times, listen for four, point the toe and tap it eight times, listen for eight.
4. Working with a partner:
   (a) Face a partner, four steps apart.
   (b) Walk forwards to partner: four steps.
       Shake right hands: four times.
       Shake left hands: four times.
       Walk backwards to starting place: four steps.
   (c) Skip forward and link right arms with a partner.
       Skip round in a circle once and back to your place: 16 steps.
   (d) Repeat (c) with left arms: 16 steps.
   (e) Skip to meet your partner, hold both hands, skip round in a circle and back to your place.
   (f) Turn away from your partner, skip away for eight steps and return for eight.

A braid dance for top infants

Have eight or ten couples in each set or use the entire class. Choose a leader couple.

1. Couples walk briskly one behind the other into a circle (sixteen steps) following the leader couple.
2. Alternate couples walk into the middle of the circle holding their braids high (eight steps).
3. These couples return to the circle walking backwards (eight steps).
4. Other couples have a turn (sixteen steps).
5. Repeat points 2, 3 and 4 (thirty-two steps).
6. The leader couple leads the other couples around the area and they all finish in a line (two in front of two, etc.).

If the children start to become competent, then other formations and movements can be suggested. You can also ask the children for ideas, for example,

1. The front couple can form an arch; all the other couples can come under the arch, turn right beyond the arch and form another line.
2. The first couple can form an arch. As each couple goes through and out of the arch they can make an arch too, until all the couples are making arches.

It is possible, with some children, eventually to try some known folk dances. But even these, in some cases, must be simplified. Appropriate ones to try are 'Pat-a-Cake Polka'; 'Cumberland Long Eight'; 'Arden Reel'; 'The Huntsmen's Chorus'. A good way to proceed is to play the music for the dance first and let the children walk, skip, or run freely to the music. Then ask them to sit down and try to clap in time to the music. The next stage is to practise the steps or body actions that will be needed for the correct execution of the dance. Lastly, teach the formation.

Pat-a-cake Polka

1. Practise jumping on the spot with two feet.
2. Practise hopping on the spot on the left leg.
3. Practise tapping the heel and then the toe in turn, first without a jump and then with a jump.
4. Practise slip steps to the right and left.
Partners:
1. Face a partner and practise slip steps together with hands joined.

2. Clap right hands, clap left hands, clap both hands.

Dance

Choose a partner. Make a circle with the boys standing with their backs to the middle, the girls facing them. Jump on the left foot four times, tap the heel and toe, heel and toe with the right foot. Join hands and slip step to the boys' right. Repeat, then slip step to the left. Clap the right hands three times, the left hands three times, both hands three times and repeat.

Cumberland long eight

1. Free practise to the music.
2. Walk to the music with bouncing steps.
3. Join hands with a partner, practise walking in the room.
4. Join right hands with a partner, shake hands. Lift hands to nose-height, practise walking around to partner's place and back to the starting position.
5. Join left hands and proceed as for point 4.
6. Make a longways set of four couples. Face your partner, shake hands.
7. Still in the set, practise making a right-hand star with the top two couples and the bottom two couples. If you give the children a number it will help! For example, couples 1, 2, 3 and 4. Corners give right hands. Number 1 lady with number 2 gentleman and number 2 lady with number 1 gentleman.

Dance

1. Single cast — the boys cast left, the girls cast right. The first couple lead and everyone follows. They walk down to the bottom of the set, then up the middle and back to their original places.
2. Double cast — the first couple turn to the right, everyone follows. They lead to the bottom of the set, up the middle and back to their original places.
3. The first and second couples join right hands, across to make

161

a star. The third and fourth couples join right hands to make a star. They walk around for eight steps.

4. Make left-handed stars and walk around for eight steps.
5. The couple at the top of the set join both hands, face each other and slip step or gallop to the bottom of the set.

Arden Reel

1. Free practice to the music.
2. Practise walking with a bouncy step.
3. Make chains of four people and practice walking around the room.
4. Find a partner, join inside hands and practise walking to the music.
5. Cross your own hands and hold your partner's hands. Walk around clockwise on the spot.

Dance

This is a longways set for four couples, each facing their partner and standing four paces away.

1. The boys join hands and the first boy leads his line all the way round the girls' line and back to their places.
2. The girls' line walks around the boys.
3. Join inside hands with your partner. Double cast — the first couple lead the other three couples out to the right, then to the bottom of the set and back to their place.
4. The second, third and fourth couples take two paces away from their partners.
5. The first couple cross their hands, hold hands and swing round and round to the bottom of the set.

The Huntsman's Chorus

1. Free practice to the music.
2. Practise walking to the music.
3. Practise slip steps to the music.
4. Face a partner and join both hands. Practise slip steps to the

music. Slip step to the right, change and slip step to the left.

5. Join inside hands and practice walking together around the room.

6. Face your partner and take two steps backwards away. Practise walking forward for three, change and back for three.

Dance

This dance requires four or six couples, partners facing one another.

1. All the girls join hands down the set, as do the boys.

2. The boys and girls move forward together to meet in the middle — forward three steps, change, backwards three steps, change.

3. The lines move forward again to meet, but this time the boys make arches and the girls go under.

4. Repeat. The lines move forwards and back and cross over.

5. Double cast — everyone follows the first couple to the bottom of the set, back up the middle and back to their places.

6. The first couple slip step halfway down the set, return to start and then slip step again, this time to the bottom of the set.

The ideas in this chapter are presented to encourage teachers to be aware of the creative experiences that can be provided for children. Wherever possible, children should be allowed freedom of response and a chance to contribute with their own ideas. Sometimes dance moves into and out of drama and needs the support of music in order to satisfy the children's creative responses. Sometimes dance moves into art and craft or vice versa and, as has already been explained, into language. Those teachers who have experienced the tingling thrill of a 'creation' which has been stimulated by dance, know how powerful this medium can be, and know the value of sharing this with children.

At the end of their time in the infant school, check whether the children can:

Work in their own space;
Stop when the music stops;
Distinguish between high and low pitch;
Follow a partner's movements, i.e. follow-my-leader;
Interpret music freely;
Understand the difference between 'right' and 'left';

Skip with the music;

Distinguish between quick and slow movements;

Move in response to different percussion sounds — movement Sensitive;

Enjoy creating movement patterns.

REFERENCES

1. K. Harrison, *Look What I Can Do!* (BBC Publications, 1986).
2. A. Bullock, *A Language for Life*, (HMSO, 1975).
3. P. Wetton, 'The Integrated Approach in the Infant School'. Paper presented to IAPESGW, Warwick University.
4. A. Utley, *The Speckled Hen*, (Collins, 1971).
5. A. Utley, *The Little Red Hen*, (Ladybird).

USEFUL READING

J. Foster, *A Very First Poetry Book* (Oxford University Press, 1984).

J. Agard, *Say it Again Granny! Twenty poems from Caribbean proverbs* (Bodley Head, 1986).

J. Pienkowski, *Sizes* (Picture Puffin, 1984).

J. Cowley, *Morning Dance* (Arnold Wheaton, 1985).

E.J.M. Woodland (ed.), *Skipping Susan, Poems for Young Children* (Bell and Hyman, 1984).

H. Lewin & L. Kipper, *Jafta* (Dinosaur Publications, 1982).

L. Thwaites, *Rosie's Wonderful Dances* (Corgi Books, 1984).

H. Nicol & J. Pienkowski, *Meg and Mog Books* (Heinemann).

R. Shreeves, *Children Dancing* (Ward Lock).

G. Cameron, Y. Conolly & St. Singham, *Mango Spice* (songs), (A. & C. Black).

Davies (Coventry), *Maypole Dance Instruction Book*, L8064/2.

MUSIC REFERENCES

Records:

M1. *Famous Marches* (HMV, ALP. 1798).

M2. *Sing a Song of Play School*, (BBC Records, REC. 212).

M3. *Capriccio Espagnol* by Rimsky Korsakov, Side One, SKATE 1.

M4. *The Nutcracker Suite, Dance of the Sugar Plum Fairy* by Tchaikovsky.

M5. *Bolero* by Ravel, Side one, SKATE 1 (MCPS).

M6. *Sing a Song of Play School.*

M7. *Barnum on Ice*, Side 2 (Safari Records).

M8. *The Greensleeves Barn Dance Singalong Dance Band* (GDB. 101).

M9. *Cassette-Country dances* (Davies of Coventry).

OTHER USEFUL MUSIC

Carnival of the Animals, Side 1, (Scholastic Publications, Decca, CE.1181).

Animal Songs, sung by David Moses, Side 2, (Scholastic Publications, Decca, CE.1181).

Seasons: Spring; Summer, Side 1 (Scholastic Publications).

Seasons: Autumn; Winter, Side 2 (Scholastic Publications).

Country Dances (Scholastic Publications).

Krazy Kreechers, (Kidsmusic, London).

Out of this World (BBC Sound Effects, REC. 225).

Maypole Dance Music Cassettes.

    Side 1: Nine Maypole Dance Tunes, Davies, Coventry, L8065/5.

    Side 2: Country dances.

Action Replay (BBC Records, REH.441).

Disco Skate, Side 2 (Safari Records).

8

Classroom Activities in the Infant School

Teacher-directed gross-motor-development activity is an essential part of the curriculum in the infant class. As a strategy, it can be developed by teachers:

1. To aid concentration.
2. To reinforce the learning of language and mathematics.
3. To compensate for the lack of indoor hall space.
4. To make 'wet playtimes' more bearable!
5. As a locus of control.

Activities which certainly aid children's concentration and have a high educational value are undoubtedly action songs and rhymes which help children not only to assimilate knowledge, but often help to motivate them into other areas of the curriculum. This kind of gross motor activity is particularly necessary for the four- and five-year-olds. Sometimes the rhymes and songs are chosen to increase the children's understanding of number or mathematical concepts. Examples of this kind of rhyme would be:

> Ten green bottles standing on the wall,
> Ten green bottles standing on the wall,
> And if one green bottle should accidentally fall,
> There would be nine green bottles standing on the wall.
> Nine green . . .

or

> Seven green speckled frogs, sat on a speckled log
> Eating the most delicious grubs, grubs, grubs,

One fell into the pool where it was rather cool,
Then there were only . . . six green . . .

Other kinds of action songs and rhymes are used by teachers to allow children to develop verbal skills and to extend their vocabulary, to help them develop muscular co-ordination and rhythmic ability and to help them to communicate. Also, by being involved in a dynamic group activity, the children learn to co-operate, to work together and to have a chance (however timid the participant), to speak out!

Wise infant school teachers organise their children's day so that a burst of activity can be followed by an activity demanding concentration and stillness. Young children find it difficult to sit still and concentrate for long periods of time and so are more ready to settle down to a sedentary activity after an active song or game. The action songs and games that are selected for classroom use will almost always have to be chosen so that the body can be active in a very confined area. Suitable rhymes would therefore be:

I'm a little teapot short	(bend down)
and stout	(spread arms, stick out tummy)
Here's my handle	(bend one arm, hand on hip)
Here's my spout	(make a spout with other arm
When I get my steam up	(pat the head with alternate hands)
hear me shout	(throw both arms high in the air)
Tip me up	(assume teapot shape, tip towards the handle)
and pour me out	(tip towards the spout)

Here stand I,	(Jump up and
Little Jumping Joan/John	down on the
When nobody's with me	spot.)
I'm all alone.	

I'm a crooked, twisted monster	(bend joints, twist spines)
With a creepy crawly hand	(bend and twist and move)
I jump up and down like this	(jump on the spot)
But watch out how I land!	(land stiff and straight)

Hop on one leg!
Hop on the other!
Shake off one foot!
Now the other!

Bend at the knees,
Bend at the waist,
Flippy-floppy monster,
See his saggy face!

The robot's arm goes chop,	(make a quick strong movement)
The robot's neck goes click,	(turn the head to one side)
Chop, click, chop, click,	(arm, head, arm, head)
The robot is going to work.	(march to places)

Incy wincey spider climbed up the water spout
    (crouch down, make climbing movements with the fingers
    and gradually stand up)
Down came the rain and washed the spider out
    (bring both arms down to sides)
Out came the sunshine and dried up all the rain
    (stretch both arms wide and high and look up)
Incy wincey spider climbed up the spout again.

'Head and shoulders, knees and toes' (See p. 144).

'Scrub your dirty face' (See p. 64).

As small as a mouse,	(curl up on the floor)
As wide as a bridge,	(stand up and stretch arms wide)
As tall as a house,	(stretch high with arms, stand on tip toes)
As straight as a pin	(stand like a soldier)

There is a collection of songs[1] written by Harriet Powell called *Game-Songs* with an accompanying cassette which is useful for use in the classroom. Try *Make a face* p. 23, *Keep on dancing*, p. 27, *The monster stomp*, p. 35, *One, two, three* p. 37, *I've got a body* p. 43, *Bendy toy*, p. 47 and *Say goodbye*, p. 63.

There are other times in some schools where practical physical considerations are equally as important as intellectual considerations. For instance, sometimes it is necessary to teach physical education lessons in the classroom. This is quite usual in some village schools and also happens occasionally in schools where perhaps structural alterations such as re-wiring or painting are taking place. On these occasions, teachers should make every effort to take children out-doors for locomotor activities, if only for five or ten minutes each day and where possible, take an outdoor PE lesson at least twice a week. Where weather conditions make this impossible, then the lesson must take place indoors. The lesson should provide the children with as much gross motor movement as possible within the space available. When indoors, teachers and children can stack the tables and chairs around the edge of the room in order to clear a space for movement.

Many of the suggestions in the chapter on dance may be adapted for classrooom use and also, many of the floorwork activities in the chapter on gymnastics. If space is very limited, it is a good idea to suggest that the children have a partner and ask them to take turns to move. Hoops are a useful aid in encouraging partners to wait patiently for their turn! Put the hoops at the edge of the room and ask the non-participants to stand or sit inside the hoop. But if this is the case, teachers should provide a good energetic warm-up first.

There are many activities that can take place on an almost static base that will exercise the body and begin to make 'all the systems go!' One such 'warm-up' session is as follows:

1. Jogging on the spot to music, until the children are 'puffing'.
2. Keeping a straight spine, slowly bend the knees and crouch down. Slowly come up to the standing position, keep the hands near the body and stretch high'. Repeat several times.
3. Clench the fists, bend the elbows and make quick alternate upward movements of the upper arm. Keep the fists in front of the face.
4. Shrug the shoulders up and down quickly.
5. Try and shake your hands off!
6. Try and shake your feet off! One at a time!
7. Wiggle your bottom!
8. Try and stand on one leg.
9. Hop on one leg.
10. Jump on the spot.

In village schools, however, where PE lessons always take place in the classroom, the teachers should try to follow the syllabus that has been agreed to and which should contain the elements already outlined in previous chapters. Where space is limited, the children can take turns on some occasions, and on others, movements can be adapted and performed in a small space. An example of how a 'general warm-up' can be linked to a gymnastic theme and adapted to limited floor space is as follows, for example, with the theme, 'Body Shape':

1. Jog on the spot. Look at your feet. Can you make them a pointed shape?
2. Stretch into a tall thin shape.
3. Twist into a twisted shape.
4. Make one arm into a straight shape and the other arm into a twisted or curled shape.
5. Stand up. Curl your upper body and limbs into a curled shape.
6. Make a bent shape.
7. Hop on one leg, keeping your other leg in a straight shape.
8. Jump on the spot and when I say 'roof', try to touch it!

But again, wherever possible, try and preface the movement training part of a lesson with locomotor activity outdoors.

Now we must consider that scourge of all infant staff rooms, the wet playtime! Wet playtimes affect the children, the staff and the whole atmosphere in the school when they occur. They therefore need analysis. Perhaps teachers should consider how they can compensate the children for the lack of exercise outdoors and the lack of free play with and without peers, which allows children 'to restore their psychic equilibrium' (S. Isaacs). Sometimes wet playtimes take place in the hall. If they are to have the desired effect however, the children would have to be allowed to play freely (supervised only for safety) or to be allowed to choose to be involved in vigorous games. Many of the 'Game-Songs' from Harriet Powell's book[1] would be useful for this kind of activity. Try *Say Hello*, p. 11, *Come to the Party*, p. 15, *Bash and Bang Band*, p. 19, *Keep on Dancing*, and *When a Dinosaur's Feeling Hungry*, p. 29, or some of the traditional 'circle' songs such as *The Okey Cokey*, or *Bobby Bingo* or *Here we go round the mulberry bush*.[2]

If wet playtimes are taken in the classroom, which is a usual scenario, particularly in certain village schools and schools disrupted by alterations, then teachers would be wise to attempt a PE lesson in the classroom immediately afterwards, before attempting to settle the children to quieter activities.

If children are not allowed some freedom from the 'conformist mode' then, as we all know, they become difficult to teach for the rest of the session. Whilst it is recognised that there is no substitute for free play in the playground, in the fresh air, these suggestions for action songs and warm-ups should help to alleviate many of the discipline problems which occur when freedom of movement is restricted. It should be obvious to the reader throughout this discussion of teacher-directed gross motor activity that implicit in all this, is the notion of control. It might be useful to end this chapter by illustrating how gross motor activity can be used as a method of control.

Some teachers use action games to gain the attention of a noisy class. The old 'Hands on Heads,' 'Hands on Shoulders, 'Hands on Knees', 'Finger on Lips', is a well-tried and well-used example of using a set of actions to gain control in the classroom, but other more interesting ones can be used once the children have learned them. Many teachers use action games such as 'Simon Says', or 'Hands and Shoulders, Knees and Toes', to help children to hurry to a carpet gathering, or to help children fill in five minutes whilst they are waiting for another class to vacate the hall, or to provide a more educational activity when they are waiting to wash their hands before lunch, etc. The following list contains other action ideas to fill in the odd five minutes or so.

Sailors (adapted version)

'Captain's coming — everybody salute.
'Scrub the deck' — on hands and knees — mime a scrubbing action.
'Climb the mainbrace' — mime climbing a rope.
'Land a-hoy' — hand on eyebrows — lean forward.
'Crabs on deck' — jump up and down on the spot.
etc.

Clapping games

Face a partner and try various clapping rhymes such as:

'My mother said' — clap both hands
'That I never should' — clap right hands
'Play with matches' — clap left hands
'In the wood.' — clap both hands.

Alphabet

The children sit on the carpet and the teacher holds up a letter, for example, the letter A. Any child with an A in their name now sits with one hand on their head. As each new letter is called the children put the other hand on their head, then stand up, then put one hand on one hip, then the other hand on the other hip, then wiggle both hands in the air, etc.

Words

Choose four words such as stand, sit, kneel and shake and write them on a card. The teacher turns her back and the children choose which action they will do. The teacher chooses one card and turns round, the children all say the name of the card 'shake'. Those children who have chosen 'shaking' are caught out!

If you have children from other countries in your classroom, this might be a good time to get them to use their native language by pointing to a part of the body and asking them what the word would be in Urdu or Benghali. I am not knowledgeable about action songs and rhymes or games from other cultures, but if the school has a policy of introducing such materials into the curriculum, then teachers can 'mix the menu' at these times. Two useful source books are *Games of the World* published by UNICEF Unit 7, Christy Industrial Estate, Kings Road, Chelmsford, Essex CM1 15B and *Let's Play Asian Children's Games*.[3]

REFERENCES

1. H. Powell, *Game-songs with Prof. Dogg's Troupe* (A. & C. Black).
2. *Learning with Traditional Rhymes* (Number, Memory, Talking, Action, Dancing, Skipping, Singing) (Ladybird Books).
3. O. Dunn, *Let's Play Asian Children's Games* (Macmillan).

OTHER RESOURCES

Action Songs and Rhymes, includes a record (Kiddicraft Ltd., 1975).
Sing a Song of Play School, record (BBC Publications).
R.A. Smith, *Blue Bell Hill Games* (Kestrel Books, 1982).
B. Ireson (ed.), *The Young Puffin Book of Verse* (Young Puffin).

9

Swimming and Water Activities (age Three to Seven)

Water safety and swimming are life skills which should be introduced to children as early as possible. We can help young children to become 'water happy' by providing a selection of water activities based primarily on self-selected free play in the home and in the pre-school, moving gradually into teacher-guided group play, both indoors and outdoors and eventually progressing to parent-teacher visits to a 'proper' swimming pool.

Parents and pre-school personnel play an important part in introducing children to water — its properties and its uses as a leisure, fun and fitness activity. It is thought, however, that developmentally there is no advantage in teaching children to swim before they are three years old, since certain considerations which affect their ability to learn, such as motor development, are not present until the age of three. There is also some concern that children under three are more subject to infection if they are exposed to swimming in public swimming pools.

Nevertheless, the foundations for the acquisition of swimming skills must be laid down as early as possible. Children need to feel happy with water and in water before being introduced to swimming and this process cannot start too early. Many parents provide opportunities for playing with water in the kitchen sink, in puddles and in the bath and many children are 'water happy' when they come to pre-school. But others are not and so it is a good idea to assume that all pre-school children may need to move through an adjustment phase. Some children, for instance, may not be ready to participate in water play at all and may resist all attempts to interest them in such activities. These children should not be forced to take part, but gently encouraged to become involved as soon as they feel confident.

Most water play in pre-schools is centred around the water

trough and is seldom related to swimming activities, but with careful planning, the children could begin to be involved in water activities that will make them more confident. The water in the trough will need to be clean and warm, and the children must be supervised by an adult if such play is to have the required effect of helping them to become 'water happy'. Adults should make all the usual preparations — put the children into waterproof aprons, roll up sleeves, etc.

SUGGESTED ACTIVITIES

1. Wiggle your fingertips on top of the water.
2. Put your fingers in the water and try and wiggle them. What does it feel like?
3. Put one hand palm down on the water, keep your hand stiff, push your hand into the water.
4. Now let your hand become floppy on top of the water. Push your hand down into the water.
5. Which way was easier, point 3 or 4?
6. Put both palms on top of the water, press down and when I say 'now', bring your hands out of the water and clap them!
7. Put both hands under the water, shoulder width apart, palms facing; try and bring your hands together under the water.
8. Put both hands together under the water, backs of hands touching, palms facing outwards, push the palms away from each other.
9. Wet one finger then touch your nose.
10. Wet one finger then touch one closed eyelid.
11. Two wet fingers, two closed eyelids.
12. Experiment and touch different parts of the face with one or two wet fingers.
13. Everybody, put your fingers in the water trough and make a little splash. Move your fingers to the middle of the trough, then to the outside of the trough, splash! splash!

In the summer months, when the weather is warmer, many pre-schools arrange different kinds of water experiences outdoors. All these experiences help children to become 'water happy'.

SUGGESTED ACTIVITIES FOR OUTDOORS

1. 'Painting' walls and fences with large brushes (such as those

used in house decorating which have been dipped in buckets of water. Let the children fill the buckets from the tap and carry them to the required site.

2. Pouring water from small containers into a larger vessel.
3. Washing dolls' clothes and hanging them on a line.
4. Blowing bubbles from pipes or plastic tubes.
5. Playing with air-flow balls in a bucket of water.
6. Controlled play with hose-pipes, e.g. watering the flowers or cleaning the yard.
7. Controlled play with squeezy bottles filled with water.
8. Making patterns on the floor with the water from a watering can or a squeezy bottle.
9. Making bubbles in a cup of water instead of drinking it!

Most pre-schools provide children with access to an inflatable paddling pool during the warmer months. This is an ideal environment to introduce children to the idea of swimming pools and swimming. Again, children need to be allowed to adapt to the water gradually. It may even be necessary, to let some children play in the pool in small groups so that they can explore and experiment in an unhurried atmosphere and overcome any fears which they might have. The most common fear for children is how the water affects their eyes, their noses and their mouths. Some children can be anxious about how to get into the pool whilst others may find difficulty in adapting to the water temperature.

SUGGESTED ACTIVITIES FOR THE TIMID CHILD IN THE PADDLING POOL

1. Practise wetting different parts of the body before going into the water — hands, cheeks, necks and tummies.
2. Practise splashing the hands in the water.
3. Rub water along the arms, tummies and legs.
4. Practise stepping into the pool and out again.
5. Stand in the water, bend your knees and try and wet your bottom!
6. Walk around the edge of the pool.
7. Play with an object in the water — a container, a watering can or a plastic ball.

SUGGESTED ACTIVITIES FOR THE CONFIDENT CHILD IN THE PADDLING POOL

1. Use the water to wet different parts of the body.
2. Get into the pool and walk about in the water.
3. Bend down and wet the bottom.
4. Sit down in the water.
5. Splash hands in the water.
6. Stand up and try to stand on one leg.
7. Practise jumping up and down on the spot.
8. Practise washing your face with the water.
9. Kneel down in the water, practise blowing a table tennis ball across the water.

The water in most inflatable paddling pools is seldom deeper than about 20 cm and in many cases no deeper than 10 cm. These are ideal depths for early swimming practices such as the ones already suggested. But children will need access to a proper swimming pool if they are to progress to the next stage. Many swimming centres have learner pools and many pre-schools arrange visits for their children. Parents should be invited to join the children so that they are encouraged to visit the centre out of school time and so that they can take part in the instructional process.

The most satisfactory type of learner pool for children of pre-school age is one which has the following characteristics:

1. A warm changing room.
2. The air temperature 1° above the water temperature.
3. The water temperature from 28°–30°C.
4. Shallow water in the entire pool and preferably no deeper than 34 cm.
5. Access by wide, shallow steps.
6. A handrail of some kind surrounding the pool.
7. A suitable range of toys — balls, inflatable ducks and fish, quoits etc.
8. At least one person in attendance competent in resuscitation procedures.

Often it is possible to arrange to have sole use of the pool. If this can be done, it is an ideal way for helping children to adapt and this should be arranged. A child's first visit to a pool can be of significant importance in making him feel happy in his surroundings and making sure he has a pleasurable experience. The whole process of a visit to a swimming centre can be quite traumatic for a young child and should, therefore, not even be attempted unless the conditions are favourable. However, a quiet, warm pool, visited with a parent, a teacher and friends is the best start that we can give the child.

Once again, do not insist that everyone goes into the water. Some timid children may not even want to change into their swimming costumes, and others will get changed and will not want to go into the water. Never force the pace. Let the child decide when he wants to go into the water. It may take four or five visits before the child feels confident to take the plunge! Let the timid child watch the other children enjoying themselves and talk to him about what the other children are doing. Encourage him to sit with his feet in the water. Invite him to go into the water with another adult. If the child enters the water, allow him to choose when he has had enough and allow him to get changed as soon as he comes out of the water. Once the timid child is in the water, he will need individual attention and should be given hand support to walk in the water. Keep the child away from boisterous friends since most timid children are upset by rough water which might splash their faces.

SUGGESTED POOL ACTIVITIES FOR CONFIDENT CHILDREN

1. Walk across the pool. Use your hands to pull the water and slide feet along the bottom.
2. Clap hands above the water.
3. Bend knees and wet your bottom.
4. Wash your face with the water. Close your eyes.
5. Sit down in the water.
6. Bend down and touch the bottom of the pool with your hand.
7. Walk on your toes across the pool.
8. Free play with balls, quoits and toys.

Do not attempt to make children put their faces in the water, or take their feet off the bottom at this stage, even though these are the two most important objectives that must be achieved if children are to learn to swim. Be patient. Keep the visits short, perhaps 15 minutes in the water. Concentrate on making the children happy. The activity must be pleasurable. Total movement in water is a strange experience for children and their initial experiences will determine how quickly they become confident in the water and how quickly they will eventually learn to swim.

The next stage is to gradually show children that the water can support the body and that the limbs can be used to propel the body through the water.

SUGGESTED ACTIVITIES FOR FUTURE VISITS TO THE SWIMMING POOL

1. Playing trains. The children line up one behind the other, perhaps eight children in a line, they hold the shoulders of the person in front and move around the pool.

2. With a partner, each child stands with his back to the pool side and faces his partner across the pool. Each child:

Walks towards his partner and shakes hands.

Walks towards his partner and claps both his hands.

Walks and changes places with his partner.

3. Partners join hands. One child stands still whilst the other practises jumping up and down on the spot.

4. Partners stand and face each other, 1 metre apart, with one table tennis ball[1] between two. One child takes a deep breath and blows the ball across the water to the other.

5. Facing a partner and standing 2 metres apart, the children practise throwing a ball to one another.

6. Facing a partner and 2 metres apart, one child walks around his partner and back to his place as quickly as possible. Each hand is used in turn to 'pull' the water away when walking.

7. Practise trying to push the water down with the palms of the hands and trying to pull the water from in front of the body, along the sides of the body, to the back of the body. Also, trying to push the water away from the front of the body.

8. Use the hands to splash the water as much as possible.

9. Bend down and touch the bottom of the pool.

10. Put both hands on the bottom of the pool.

11. Crawl along on hands and feet on the bottom of the pool.

12. Put both hands on the bottom of the pool and take a deep breath. Close your mouth and eyes and without breathing, put your face into the water.

13. As for point 12 but with your eyes open. 'Can you see your hands?'

14. Put your hands on the bottom of the pool and stretch one leg

out behind you. 'Can you move around the pool?' Practise taking a breath and blowing the air out across the water as you walk.

15. Put water into your cupped hands, take a big breath in through your mouth and blow the water out of your hands.

16. Take a deep breath and blow bubbles into the water.

17. Take a deep breath, close your mouth, put your head in the water and hum a tune.

18. Take a deep breath, close your mouth, put your head under the water, blow all the air out, come up, take another breath, etc.

19. Put both hands on the bottom of the pool, with the head clear of the water. Extend the body, lift both legs off the bottom, then propel the body by walking on the hands with the legs trailing behind.

20. As for point 19, but encourage the children to kick their legs. N.B. Some children may need the support of inflated arm bands at this stage, but these should not be offered to them too early. Let the children try without bands first.

21. Some children will eventually move about so competently that their hands and arms will begin to describe a dog-paddle action. N.B. Children feel safe in shallow water because there is no problem about regaining an upright position. They can easily kneel on the floor of the pool with their heads above water.

22. Sit on the floor of the pool with your hands on the floor and keep your arms straight, stretching your legs out and pushing on your hands. Gentle pressure on the hands will cause the legs to rise towards the surface.

23. As for point 22 but using the hands to walk backwards.

24. As for point 23 but trying to kick the legs up and down gently.

Only a small proportion of infant school children receive swimming lessons as a curricular activity during school hours. Amongst those children who do have lessons, however, there will be many children who will not have visited a pool before. Therefore, the same careful, sensitive approach and adjustment period should be adopted as has already been described for pre-school children and wherever possible, the children should have access to a shallow pool in the early stages. Where children are taken to a larger learner pool with deeper water, the following stages are recommended:

THE EARLY STAGES OF TEACHING IN A LARGE POOL

1. The physical conditions must be suitable as indicated previously.
2. The teacher should have a recognised swimming qualification, which will include a competence in resuscitation.
3. Wherever possible, infant children should be taught by their class teacher. Where this is not possible, she should always be in attendance.
4. Children who need arm bands should be fitted with them by the class teacher.
5. The depth of the water should be no deeper than mid-chest height.
6. If the depth of the pool varies, a rope should be suspended across the pool to show the children the boundary of their water space.
7. Children should be shown which is their water space and the use of the whistle as a signal for the class to stop, look and listen should be explained.
8. Teach the children how to enter the pool by the steps provided. 'Face the steps, hold the rails with both hands and place the feet carefully on the steps. Step down backwards into the pool'.
9. 'Hold the rail or trough and walk carefully along the side of the pool'.
10. Progress to using the 'water-happy' practices previously described. Be patient! Keep the children moving so that they keep warm and encourage them to keep their shoulders under the water.

Information about the teaching of swimming strokes is covered clearly, accurately and comprehensively in the book *The Teaching of Swimming* which may be obtained from: A.S.A. Headquarters, Harold Fern House, Derby Square, Loughborough, Leicester, LE11 0AL. Infant teachers should, however, keep a balance between the formal teaching of swimming strokes and play activities in the water. Many of the games we play in school can be adapted to the water and children often find more pleasure, gain more confidence and eventually learn to swim more quickly if teachers keep a firm approach in the water in these early years.

REFERENCES

1. Egg flips (a substitute for table tennis balls), other play toys and safety

aids may be obtained from: The Swim Shop, 52 Albert Road, Luton, Beds. LU1 3PR.

USEFUL BOOKS

The Teaching of Swimming (The Amateur Swimming Association, 1981).
Babes in the Water (Swimming Times Publications Ltd.).
Teaching of Swimming for those with Special Needs (Swimming Times Publications Ltd.).

10

Children with Special Needs

The Education Act (1981) 'Education of Handicapped Children' came into force in April 1983. It abolished the former categories of handicap and focused instead on the children's abilities and their interaction with the environment, rather than on their handicap. Thus handicapped children now became children with 'special needs' and 'mainstreaming' became a new term in our educational vocabulary.[1]

My purpose in this chapter is to draw attention to the physical needs of children with disabilities who used to attend special schools but who are now functioning in normal schools. Specific information about some common disabilities will be given towards the end of the chapter, but at the outset, it is important to remember that there have always been some children in normal schools who have special needs. These children were integrated into normal schools before the 1981 Education Act became law. They were children who were variously ignored or helped, depending on the easy identification of their disability and of course on how much information had been given to the teacher by parents and other agencies. Those who were easy to identify were those with disabilities such as cystic fibrosis, asthma, epilepsy, diabetes and the mildly affected spastics. Those who were less easily identified were the slightly maladjusted, the mildly visually and hearing impaired children and perhaps, most of all, those who might be called 'clumsy' children. Now that the 1981 Act has become law, however, teachers are required to be more aware of all the disabilities of children and to provide programmes that will allow children with differing special needs to work effectively alongside and with other children in physical education lessons. Thus, by implication, teachers are required to be more knowledgeable about how to respond to children with these special conditions.

Many class teachers, however, are fearful of accepting children with disabilities into their classes. This is understandable, particularly in the early years. Most of us have been trained in a system which formerly gave specialist attention to these children and we are aware that a whole range of different kinds of people supported the staff in specialist schools. Suddenly, however, we are now expected to cope alone! Consequently, we may feel inadequate. This should not be the case. Early childhood educators are probably more aware of the needs of children, whether they are disabled or not, than other groups of teachers, since they are constantly in contact with the same children throughout the whole time that the children are in school or pre-school. Most of our early childhood establishments, and particularly nurseries and play groups, base their work on the needs of the child rather than on the activity. The ethos of early-childhood communities is created around a child-centred philosophy which allows children to develop at their own rates of learning. This, I would suggest, is an ideal environment for the integration into school of children with disabilities.

The teacher, however, as always, is central to the success and happiness of the disabled children in her care. It is the teacher's attitude which is so important if these children are to be acceptable within the group. The teacher's attitude is also crucial to the disabled child's self-image. Obviously then, we need to awaken teachers' perceptions about disabled children. Unfortunately some teachers tend to be more sympathetic to children with particular kinds of abilities, and visibly withdrawn from others. The teacher's visible behaviour can have a negative effect on a disabled child's concept of self and on the other children's behaviour towards him. Much can be achieved, both for the child with a disability and the children around him, if the teacher shows good common sense in her interaction with both the disabled child and his peers. It is sometimes difficult for teachers to resist giving too much attention to, or doing too much for, certain disabled children. This is particularly so with children having physical handicaps and those who suffer visual impairment. Such temptations must be resisted. All disabled children must be helped to cope with their disability and so must those around them. Most disabled children settle and respond well to mainstream schooling if they are allowed to learn how to use their bodies to best effect in a natural and normal setting.

Teachers should be reassured too and should feel safe with the knowledge that children who would have normally attended special school prior to the 1981 Act will have been identified and their needs assessed prior to school entry. Thus, before the child enters school, a dialogue should have taken place between the school, the parents, the health authorities and support agencies, so that the teacher is fully aware of the needs of the child who is to come into her care. This should develop into a continuous dialogue if the child is to progress.

It is important (particularly for pre-school teachers) to note, that not all children with special needs are expected to be placed in mainstream establishments. Most local authorities accepted a policy of putting children with disabilities into 'the least restrictive environment', particularly since the 1981 Act made it clear that fulfilling the educational needs of disabled children should not damage the needs of normal children. Teachers should plan with this in mind. It should be remembered too, 'that the 1981 Act places an obligation on LEAs to ensure that adequate provision is made for all pupils with special education needs,'[2] and that where such a child is present in school, extra staffing must be provided.

Schools can, however, help all the children, including the disabled, by planning ahead so that some of the obvious problems are alleviated.

PRE-PLANNING

1. Be aware of the child/children's disability.
2. Collect all available information about the particular condition.
3. Plan programmes which concentrate on the child's ability, not his disability.
4. Plan enjoyable, easily attainable activities initially, so that the child gains confidence.
5. Evaluate the physical environment. Will the child's disability limit his locomotion? Is it necessary to rearrange the facilities? Are any ramps, grab rails, etc., needed?
6. Think of ways of adapting the provision of physical play, so that the child can be independent when self-selecting play. Is any special equipment needed?
7. Do you need any specialist help?
8. Would another adult be helpful?
9. Do you need to give extra information to the other children so that the disabled child is safe?
10. Do you need to consider using more descriptive language and more visible body language so that the child experiences success?
11. How will you monitor his progress?
12. How can you encourage the child to be independent, to make his own decisions and to understand his own abilities?

There are now many books available which give guidance to teachers about specific disabilities and the ways of helping children to develop their abilities to the full. The following information is a guide to help students and teachers to begin to cope with disabled children in mainstream situations when teaching physical education.

THE NURSERY AND PLAY GROUP

Adequate provision must be made when children with special needs are integrated into nurseries and play groups. The best kind of provision and the most important one, is to increase the adult-child ratio accordingly. Children with disabilities need to feel wanted and accepted within their own communities. They need to develop a positive self-image and need to feel normal. The more help they can receive from knowledgeable and patient adults in the early stages, the less chance there will be of damaging their personalities because of bad planning or lack of care.

The next step is to consider how to encourage the child to be independent. In free-play sessions, allow the child to choose his own play, intervene only when necessary, as with any other child. Compensate for any lack of physical experiences during the planned PE programme (see Chapter 4).

During such a programme, it will be possible to place special emphasis on certain activities in order to help children with disabilities. The specialist activities should be planned after consultation with the parents and medical experts and after seeking out printed materials from the specialist organisations. (Some source material is suggested at the end of the chapter.) It must be remembered too, that children with disabilities are as different from one another as normal children, even within one category of disability.

Groups of children can be clustered for specialist activities. Wherever possible, do not isolate the disabled child except where expert physiotherapy or specialist guidance is being provided from support agencies. Organise the nursery or playgroup so that all the children have a planned group session at some time during the week, not just those with special needs. If the children are grouped according to their needs, then the physically handicapped child in a wheelchair can be physically active alongside a clumsy child or an undeveloped child or a normal child. It is not only the disabled children, but all the children who can benefit from concrete practical experience and ordered stimulation since any delay in sensory information can limit cognitive and motor development and cause retardation in the developing brain and body.

When children are working in small groups with the teacher, target activities can be created by the teacher and be repeated by the children so that individual observation and communication is possible. Use should be made of auxiliaries and student teachers during this time so that children can be observed and evaluated satisfactorily. However, unqualified staff should never be involved in specialist PE activities at any stage unless the teacher has given specific guidance and has given specific instructions about the aim of the activity and how to approach it.

Arrange the planned specialist group activities to accommodate all the children. Asthmatic children, for instance, need to warm up gently before being involved in cardio-vascular type activities and need relaxing gaps between later strenuous or chasing activities. Children with other disabilities such as epileptics and the visually and hearing impaired also need rests between energetic activities, but so do we all! So follow the golden rule for all strenuous activities at this stage — alternate a hectic activity with a static one.

Children with special needs can be categorised into four main groups:

1. Children with physical disabilities.
2. Children with sensory handicaps.
3. Children with moderate learning difficulties.
4. Children with emotional or behavioural disorders.

(Allonby, 1985)

Physically handicapped children

1. Concentrate on exercising the parts of the body which are mobile.
2. Provide experiences which allow the child to practise whatever skills they have.

Adapt equipment if necessary. A bigger, softer ball? A heavier ball? A lighter or wider bat? A lower/higher target? A tricycle that can be manipulated with the hands only?

Visually impaired children[3]

1. Have an intervention programme. The children will need help with listening skills and with building up a PE vocabulary or a functioning vocabulary.
2. Help the children to 'feel' their way across apparatus and to listen to sounds.
3. Guide the children across the outdoor and indoor environment. Let them feel surfaces. Let them feel their way and 'listen' their way towards storage places for balls, tricycles, carts, etc.
4. Let them run freely in the outdoors when other children are indoors in the early stages.
5. Let them practise dressing and undressing themselves for PE lessons.
6. Use a ball with a tinkling bell inside.
7. Use larger balls with specific colours and/or textures.
8. Encourage the other children to say the child's name when joining him or inviting him to play.

Hearing-impaired children[4]

1. Speak clearly and face the child. Use body language. Do not exaggerate mouth movement or speed of speech. Make other children aware of the need to tap the child, then face him to speak.
2. Use a drum in movement sessions, or beat on the floor to help the child hear/feel the rhythm. If necessary, hold the child's hand and move with him.
3. Encourage the child to use large apparatus such as slides, trikes, trucks, etc. and talk to him as much as possible as he moves.

Children with moderate learning difficulties

1. Encourage the child to have large motor experiences — rough-and-tumble, climbing, sliding, balancing, playing with toys with wheels. Keep him moving as much as possible. Give him plenty of praise and reassurance. Build his confidence.
2. Observe him carefully by asking such questions as: 'Have you had a turn on the tricycle today?' 'I haven't seen you climbing, can I come and watch you'? 'Would you like a turn on the slide? I will hold your hand.'

Children with emotional and behavioural disorders

Physical activity can be used both by staff and children to turn negative behaviour into positive behaviour. However, there are so many different problems that children can present, that teachers must seek specialist guidance at the earliest opportunity. For example, for some children, free access to the outdoors or rough-and-tumble play can help them at difficult times. For other children, a tightly structured programme is more suitable.

INFANT SCHOOL

Disabled children who attend mainstream schools should not be excluded from physical education lessons. Children with disabilities need more physical education than normal children, to compensate for any retardation caused by their disability. Children who have been processed through the statementing procedures should have ancillary help in addition to the teacher.

Children who normally receive their education in a special unit attached to the school often join children of their age group for physical education lessons. Again, these children should be accompanied by an ancillary helper or a specialist member of staff. Some children, particularly the visually impaired will join mainstream physical education lessons and will, in addition, receive extra physical education in the special unit.

Teachers should always plan positively for these children. For instance, if the class is practising soccer skills, a ball with a bell inside or a ball which plays a tune (Mettoy toys) will be most helpful. Sometimes, sight impaired children have problems with recognising specific colours or with tracking objects. It is important therefore, to find out which colour of ball is more readily seen by each child or indeed if a patterned ball might be better. Experienced teachers have also covered targets and bats with silver foil to make tracking easier. It is also more motivating to throw at targets which make a noise when hit, (e.g. a tin bucket) rather than aiming at a hoop or a basket!

For the child who is without the use of his legs or feet, be sensible during soccer activities, and adapt his skill practices. Suggest that he practises with a bat alongside his wheelchair, or give him and a friend alternative practices, for example, goalkeeping. He will be able to be goalkeeper of course, if you narrow the goalmouth and allow him to use a bat to extend his reach!

In group work, make sure that the disabled child is an asset and not a hindrance to the group. Do not set targets that he cannot achieve. The disabled child should, however, be expected to work hard and put as much effort as possible into practising skills as a normal child.

The hearing-impaired child should be able to perform all the activities that are within the reach of children with normal hearing. Some deaf children have certain problems with balance, as do some sight-impaired children, but the chief problem with this disability is communication. The teacher should always face the child with a hearing problem and get eye contact to ensure that he is lip reading. In dance, if reproduced sound is being used, the child should be allowed to work as near as possible to the sound source. Other children can be used for supplementary help. Body language, particularly hand signalling, is a reliable aid.

Children who are mentally retarded should be accepted at their present level of performance. Praise and encouragement should be given constantly. Teachers should use a positive approach and give a positive emphasis to lower-order skills which will give success. These children derive a great deal of benefit from physical activities once they have the confidence to take part. Sometimes, retarded children are classified as lazy and fat and categorised as not being able to do this or that, when often, they have not been given enough attention or stimulation. Many retarded children reach very high standards of co-ordination, strength and agility when given enough practice. Retarded children can also exhibit aesthetic awareness when encapsulated in recorded music, quite unbelieved by those who have not seen it previously. Before the child can achieve this, however, he needs a warm, patient and understanding teacher who makes her instructions clear, simple and short and who makes sure that the child knows what is expected of him. Body language can play an important part in his learning process too.

It is important to the progress of disabled children that the other children become aware of and are sympathetic to their limitations. Normal children may need some help and guidance from the teacher, particularly about when assistance might be needed or might be definitely unwanted. Pity is to be avoided. The greatest achievement for the disabled child or any other child is, of course, when the child becomes part of the gang!

To summarise:

1. Identify the need.

2. Gather background information.
3. Establish objectives.
4. Keep records.
5. Emphasise ability not disability.

Finally, early childhood educators, but in particular, infant teachers, should be aware that physical education is regarded as an important part of the total development of disabled children and that they should be exposed to at least one period of PE each day.

A list of some of the most common disabilities that may be found in our younger children follows. It is not exhaustive and can only be superficial in a text of this nature. Teachers are recommended to seek out detailed information from the recognised specialist organisations and specialist texts that are suggested at the end of this chapter.

SOME COMMON DISABILITIES

Amputation

Usually, amputees are able to function in physical activities without much additional support other than a friendly query every so often.

Arthritis

Participation depends on the severity of the condition. There is usually a lack of general mobility, particularly in the fingers. The child should always be included in activities and allowed to exercise within his capabilities.

Asthma

This is brought on by the child's sensitive lungs reacting to different kinds of irritants. An attack is brought on when the airways in the lungs become narrow and inflamed, preventing proper breathing. Allergies range from dust, pollen and animals to cold air, smoke and exercise! Even normal feelings such as excitement or anger can cause a problem. But the message is, 'Educate the child on how to cope with an attack, how to use a relevant drug, and how to exercise to be strong to cope with an attack.' If children and their parents can begin to understand the nature of their treatment and take the relevant drug correctly, then attacks can be avoided. Teachers will need to have close consultations with the child's parents and doctor before including him in an exercise programme. Teachers can help the child to take the correct medication prior to exercise if given clear instructions. Asthmatics should take part in the normal PE programme because they need to increase their tolerance to exercise, to improve their muscle power and to improve their cardio-vascular performance, perhaps even more than normal children.

Cystic fibrosis

Such children should be treated as normal. They gain positive benefits from physical activity.

Diabetes

Staff should be aware of insulin reactions and diabetic comas, but diabetic children should take part in all activities unless specifically excluded or restricted by a doctor.

Epilepsy

The teachers should find out the full details of each child's condition, since it is dangerous to generalise. In some people, for instance, seizures (fits) only occur twice a year, in others, twice a day, in some, only in sleep and in some, not at all, because the condition is controlled effectively by medication. Many children can be treated normally and can be included in PE activities. The child who has a seizure in school may need special attention. For partial seizures, where the child's consciousness seems clouded, then keen observation will have prevailed and the child can be guided to a safe place for a few minutes. Where children suffer from petit mal, i.e. where they 'switch-off' for a couple of seconds, there should be a 'buddy' system adopted if the child goes swimming with his class and the child should not climb high up on apparatus. For generalised convulsions, keep the child from injuring himself and then reassure and comfort him after the convulsion is over. For generalised convulsions in which consciousness is not regained, then a doctor should be summoned immediately. Epileptics can often detect the onset of an attack and should be allowed to retreat to a quiet corner at once. Children with epilepsy can do most of the activities that other children become involved in and can be included in group games and swimming. Most of them can also climb and hang on large items of apparatus (depending on their condition). The most important aspect of school life for epileptics is to be accepted as 'normal'. Their self-image can be permanently damaged in mainstream education if they are excluded from PE and if their teachers and peers make them seem different.[5]

Spina bifida[6]

'These children often have normal intelligence but may have other handicaps such as varying degrees of paralysis, perhaps some sensory loss and bowel and bladder incontinence and often hydrocephalus' (Lauder et al., 1978). The child will normally have specialist help within the school system and should, therefore, be included in PE activities. The support worker (or parent) will work alongside the teacher and adapt the activities and encourage the child when necessary.

Muscular dystrophy

In the early stages, the child should be included in activities as a normal child. As the condition progresses, the child should be regularly assessed and support should be provided as soon as it becomes necessary.

Modern learning difficulties

Children who are mildly retarded often have motor problems and can therefore benefit greatly from physical education activities. The teacher will need a great deal of patience, however, and her speech will need to be clear when giving verbal instructions. The teacher will also need to give individual attention to the child to stimulate and motivate him to move. He must be encouraged to try and if necessary, be led, if he is to achieve. Praise and encouragement will help, but the teacher needs to set goals for him and insist that he achieves them.

Clumsy children[2]

'No one has yet come up with a definition of such a child, or a foolproof way of assessing whether or not a child fits this category'. (M. Gallagher, 1986). Gordon and McKinley (1980) attempted a description:

'Such children are often delayed in learning even the simpler movements such as walking and running, and have great difficulty in learning to use their hands and to copy motions shown to them. They are slow in learning to dress themselves and are clumsy in their attempts to button their clothes, tie their laces, handle a spoon and in other simple tasks'.

Gallagher suggests that in an ideal environment, 'a simple screening test for motor problems could be carried out at around six years of age to identify children who may be "at risk" of developing other learning problems'. He also suggests a check list that teachers could use:

Have you come across a child who:
1. Is always last to be 'chosen' in team games.
2. When allocated to a team is greeted with groans.
3. Regularly spills milk, water, etc.
4. Regularly breaks pencils.
5. Fumbles with and drops small apparatus such as pegs.
6. Constantly falls in the playground and boosts school consumption of plasters.
7. Is a messy and slow eater.
8. Is a messy and slow dresser.
9. Gets involved in frequent minor 'scuffles' caused by accidentally bumping or knocking others.
10. Produces smudgy, untidy work and has difficulty with writing.
11. 'Clowns' his way through school.
12. Is always on the periphery at playtimes.
13. Walks into things when crossing the classroom (chairs, desks or people!).

Not every child will display all these traits and it is possible that in pre-school, he displays none of them because he has already withdrawn from the activities that cause him embarrassment. Careful observation by the adult can be crucial to him since there is more chance of help with motor problems in the pre-school situation than in the infant school. He will need to be encouraged to be more involved in gross, fine and locomotor activities with the active support of an adult. The clumsy child is often immature in relation to motor development and will need to have the skills taught by breaking them down into easier stages and may even need to go back to first principles. Severe cases should receive specialist group PE activities and specialist physiotherapy treatment.

Effects of clumsiness on the child

1. Lack of status and significant skills (throwing, catching, kicking), leads to lack of social interaction with the peer group.
2. Lack of mobility in the shoulder, arm, wrist and fingers leads to difficulties in handling small apparatus and therefore activities such as writing, drawing, painting, building, etc.
3. Retardation of perceptual motor development leads to poor academic performance in number, reading, etc.
4. Lack of ability to complete skills such as dressing, sorting, carrying, walking etc., leads to a lack of confidence and self-esteem.
5. Teacher tension is apparent, which leads to withdrawal symptoms.
6. Eventual emotional and behavioural problems are present.

REFERENCES

1. L. Groves, *Physical Education for Special Needs* (Cambridge University Press, 1979).
2. L. Groves, (ed.) *Who Cares? A Collection of short articles for caring Physical Educationalists* (PEA, 1985).
3. D. Tooze, *Independence Training for Visually Handicapped Children*, (Croom Helm, 1981).
4. Groves, *Who Cares?*
5. S. McGovern, British Epilepsy Association, 1985.
6. Lauder *et al.* 'Educational placement of Children with Spina Bifida', *Exceptional Children*, 45, 437–7 (1978).

USEFUL READING

A. Brown, *Active Games for Children with Movement Problems* (Harper and Rowe, 1987).
S. Curtis (ed.), *From Asthma to Thalassaemia: Medical conditions in*

Childhood. British Agencies for Adoption and Fostering, 11 Southwark Street, London SE1, 1RQ, 1986.

DES, *Young Children with Special Educational Needs* (HMSO, 1983) An HMI survey of educational arrangements made in 61 nurseries.

DES, *Physical Education for the Physically Handicapped* (HMSO, 1971).

B. Gillham (ed.), *Handicapping Conditions in Children* (Croom Helm, 1986).

N. Gordon & I. McKinlay (eds.), *Helping Clumsy Children* (Churchill Livingstone, 1980).

C.R. Musselwhite, *Adaptive Play for Special Needs Children* (Taylor and Francis, 1985). (Particularly useful for pre-school teachers.)

PEA, *Physical Education and Recreation for People with Special Needs, An Annotated Bibliography* (1986). 162 Kings Cross Road, London.

Physical Education for Pupils with Special Needs, Kent Education Authority.

L. Routledge, *Only Child's Play* (Heinemann Books, 1978).

OTHER USEFUL ADDRESSES

British Diabetic Association, 10 Queen Anne Street, London, W1M OBD.

National Society for Epilepsy, Chalfont Centre for Epilepsy, Chalfont St. Peter, Gerrards Cross, Buckinghamshire, SL9 0RJ.

Royal National Institute for the Blind, 224 Great Portland Street, London W1N 6AA.

The Royal National Institute for the Deaf, 105 Gower Street, London WC1E 6AH.

UK Sports Association for People with Mental Handicap, Hayward House, Bernard Crescent, Aylesbury, Buckinghamshire, HP21 9PP.

11

Resources, Storage and Supplies

If the objectives for pre-school and infant school physical education are to be achieved, there must be adequate resources. There should be enough equipment provided so that both indirect and direct learning can take place. Freedom of choice in play is an important part of the developmental process in young children: riding a bike, pushing and pulling a truck, climbing, ball play . . . and in order for learning to take place, there must be enough equipment for the children to use. All children must have sufficient material to encourage the use of large and small muscles so that they can assemble information about the physical world. There is also a necessity in infant schools (even though formalised timetables preclude free-choice play), to have a policy about equipment, certainly in lessons with small apparatus based on the 'one-for-one' principle, so that all children can have 'hands-on' experience.

It seems to make good sense in pre-schools to elect one person to be responsible for physical education equipment. In infant schools, the curriculum leader for PE will take the responsibility. The need for an inventory of all equipment in use is important for many reasons. Not only can equipment be checked and counted at the beginning and end of each year, but an accurate inventory will allow the replacement of items and an efficient repair system to be established.

All personnel involved in the educational process at this level should decide as a team what they consider to be a basic list of equipment for their children and gradually build up their stock. In state schools, the larger items are often supplied by the PE adviser and any additional items are often not forthcoming in these bleak economic times. However, pressure should still be brought to bear on the adviser if there is a concensus amongst the staff that a certain item of equipment is necessary for the physical development of their children.

Any equipment purchased should be of good quality and obtained from a reputable manufacturer. Apparatus should always be the correct size and weight for children of different age groups. Nursery equipment, for instance, should be smaller and lighter than equipment for top infants. Similarly, apparatus which is suitable for top juniors must be adapted for use with reception class children. It may be necessary therefore, to buy adjustable equipment. Several suggestions for suitable supplies are listed at the end of this chapter.

SUGGESTED BASIC SUPPLIES — INFANT SCHOOL

Gymnastics

1. A foldaway climbing frame — height 3 metres (with ropes attached).
2. A nest of stacking agility tables of three different heights with coloured, padded tops.
3. Two portable folding climbing frames with bridging equipment — 2 trestles (2 metres high) 1 ladder, 1 balance beam 1 padded plank, 1 wooden plank
4. Four balance benches — 2.75 m x 30 cm with a wide top and a balance facility underneath.
5. Six agility mats — 1.2 m x 1.8 m with vinyl surfaces and in different colours.
6. A safety mattress — 1.2 m x 1.8 m and at least 20 cm thick.
7. One individual mat per child in four colours (92 cm x 40 cm x 12 mm).

Other interesting items

1. Geometric mats — four colours and four different shapes — circular, square, oblong and hexagonal.
2. A movement table — a circle, 92 cm in diameter, with a padded top on four legs with linking bars at different heights.
3. A bar box — a padded oblong top on telescopic legs with two linking bars on each side, 70 cm to 102 cm.
4. A bar stool — a padded square top on four metal legs, each linked by three bars, heights 86 cm and 106 cm.

5. A wobble board — a red wooden circular board on centrally placed wheels, 60 cm in diameter.

Basic supplies for games

These are listed on pp. 51 and 135.

Basic supplies for dance

1. A record player — a solid structure with three speeds and good quality speakers.
2. A tape recorder — a solid structure with a cassette facility, and a tape counter.
3. Chime bars.
4. A drum.
5. A tambourine.
6. A triangle.
7. Cymbals.
8. Maracas.
9. Castanets.
10. Blank tapes.
11. Tapes and records — build up a library of suitable music. Suggestions: *The Peer Gynt Suite* (Grieg), *The Carnival of Animals* (Sain-Saens), *The Planets* (Holst), *BBC Sporting Themes* (BBC records), *The Children's Corner Suite* (Debussy), music from *The Sting* (Scott Joplin) and *In Dulce Jubilo* (Mike Oldfield).

Other basic supplies

1. Playground chalk.
2. A stopwatch.

Other interesting items (modern rhythmic gymnastics)

1. Balls, 69 mm in diameter, with a special finish for a superb grip.
2. Ribbons, single-sided satin, 5 cm wide, 4.5 m long and double thickness for the first metre.

198

STORAGE

It is essential for the good management of all lessons, that equipment and supplies should be systematically stored in a central area. Everything should have a place and all personnel should return it to that place so that each person can have immediate access to the equipment at the beginning of each lesson. Shelves should be labelled to assist staff in replacing items in the correct place and all items should have either a shelf space or a floor space which is known to all staff, (in an effort to increase efficiency).

Small items of games equipment and percussion instruments used to be the most difficult to store because of the size and number of the items, but recently sports suppliers and educational suppliers have produced some very useful containers, nets and container trolleys on wheels in an effort to help personnel in schools. There is a very wide range of containers now available. Most of them are made of brightly coloured, plastic-coated wire and are available in many different shapes and sizes. Some of the baskets have handles and can be stacked on top of each other, either on the floor or on a shelf, whilst others stack in various ways onto trolleys. There are also specialised stands with and without wheels for storing hoops, specialised trolleys for storing gymnastic mats and yet another type for storing percussion instruments.

Gymnastic benches can be stored around the sides of the hall and mats can either be stacked neatly in a pile in one corner, or stored in a vertical mat trolley in order to create space in the PE alcove or store. If these items are stored in the PE store, they often prevent access to other items. Mats are a necessary but expensive item and should be handled with great care. Never allow children to drag them across the floor and do not allow them to be used for non-PE activities. Mats can easily be torn with a sharp heel or a metallic toy.

All PE equipment should be checked at regular intervals for wear and tear. Large hinges on apparatus and bolts and hooks should be checked even more regularly and taken out of use if damaged. The tops of benches and vinyl covered tables should be cleaned with a mild disinfectant. So too, should plastic balls, hoops, quoits and gymnastic mats. Balls should be inflated to their proper pressure and children should be encouraged not to sit on them! Bats should be checked regularly for any splinters and children should be discouraged from using them as hammers for 'knocking in' wickets, etc. If splinters do appears, then the bats should be taped.

SOME SUPPLIERS OF NURSERY AND
PRIMARY EQUIPMENT

Nottingham Educational Supplies,
17 Ludlow Hill Road, West Bridgford, Nottingham NG2 6HD
This company has a comprehensive range of games and gymnastic equipmment which is ideal for use in pre-schools and infant schools. All the apparatus listed here is available in four colours: red, green, yellow and blue.
The games apparatus includes:

1. Vinyl-coated foam balls in four different sizes, some with a low bounce that would be suitable to help timid or handicapped children who have poor or slow co-ordination.
2. Bean bags, quoits, hoops, short tennis racquets, and a stack of 40 multi-markers.

The gymnastic equipment includes:

1. Agility mats — 4ft x 3ft, PVC-covered, with a high density. They are flame retardant.
2. Nesting agility tables — 2ft, 2ft 6in, 3ft, 3ft 6in and 4ft high.
3. 'Rough-and-tumble' safety landing mattresses (blue only), 4ft x 8ft x 8in.

This company also produces the 'Warwick' range of nursery equipment, consisting of 15 items mostly manufactured from high quality timber. The pieces are designed to cope with smaller bodies, and are easily transported.
The range includes: a horizontal bar, a slide, a timber bar, a swing, an aluminium alloy pole, a plank with battens, a balance bench, a plank with hooks, a ribbed bar box, three trestles, heights 3ft 9in, 4ft 9in, x 8ft 9in, also, a balance beam on blocks and a folding climbing frame with rungs, a slide and two platforms. The last two items would be most suitable for use in reception and nursery classrooms.
The swimming equipment includes:

1. Play bricks in four colours, 18 cm x 9 cm x 4.5 cm, which will float.

2. Sinkers with coloured rings, weighted to stand vertically on the pool bottom.
3. Aids for the handicapped — swim rings, specially adapted for ages 2–6 years, swim collars to give head support, a training belt with rings and rope.

Continental Sports Paddock, Huddersfield, West Yorkshire.

This firm has a comprehensive and creative range of gymnastic equipment which has been specially designed for primary school use and has been one of the leaders in the field of foldaway climbing frames and space-saving apparatus, such as nesting agility tables. The equipment includes:

1. Nesting agility tables, heights — 2ft, 2ft 6in, 3ft, 3ft 6in and 4ft, which are sold separately or in sets. The padded tops are available in the four colours,
2. Bar box, agility stool,
   circular movement table,
   wobble board and bench
   — Tall tops available in
   four colours: red, green,
   yellow and blue.
3. Foldaway climbing frames in a choice of 6 different gate patterns. Height 12in.
4. Portable climbing and   Trestles (folding) 3ft, 6ft, 8ft
   bridging equipment. —   Ladder 7ft, 8ft and 9ft
        Single pole 7ft, 8ft and 9ft
        Double pole, 7ft
        Balance beam, 7ft
        Padded plank, 7ft
        Timber plank, 9ft
5. Individual mats — 36in x 16in x ½in in four bright colours. (Are particularly recommended by teachers who work with children with special needs.)
6. Geometric mats —   Circle 4ft in diameter, square 4ft x 4ft, oblong 5ft x 3ft, hexagon, approximately, in four colours.
7. Mat trolleys —   Vertical, small size, 4ft x 3ft, PVC coated, flame retardant
8. Safety mattress —   6ft x 4ft x 4in, blue only, with a PVC anti-slip base.

201

9. Duflex agility mats —   2 m x 1 m x 3 cm,
                             PVC coated, fire retardant,
                             blue only.

Evans, Mercury House, Sutherland Road, Longton,
Stoke-on-Trent, ST3 1JD.

This firm has a range of equipment which could be used in the
nursery and infant school.

The range includes:

1. Plastic hoops —   Polypropylene moulded for safety in
                            four bright colours and four sizes.
                            18in, 24in, 30in and 36in in
                            diameter.
2. Multi-markers —   Heavy duty plastic. 8in dome-shaped
                            discs (40) stackable. In yellow,
                            white, blue and red.
3. Equipment   Polythene coated wire-mesh con-
    container —   tainer with lockable lid, drop-down
                            front panel and nylon wheels. 36in x
                            24in x 27in.
4. Equipment trolley —   With four detachable baskets (four
                            colours) with hoop storage and
                            bat/cane storage fitting 41in x 28in
                            x 28in.

The water-play equipment includes:

Play bricks —   Brightly coloured blocks suitable for
                            play pools. 18 cm x 9 cm x 4.5 cm.
                            Set of 24.
Armbands —   Infants size 0 and size 1.
Arm discs —   Children's size.
Play balls —   Teamsters — 9 mm. in diameter in
                            four colours.

The gymnastic equipment includes:

Individual mats —   In four bright colours, 36in x 18in
                            x ¾ in.

Hestair Hope Ltd., St. Phillips's Drive, Royston, Oldham,
OL2 6AG.

This company has possibly the most comprehensive range of
apparatus for movement, which not only includes the usual range of
games and gymnastic equipment but some specialised equipment for
children with special needs. The company also produce some creative

items such as Quadro, Combi, etc., together with womblers, ball pools, parachutes and turtle and oyster water and sand containers. The games equipment includes:

1.	Activity skittles —	Plastic coated wire, in four bright colours, height 457mm.
2.	Marker cones —	Similar to 'traffic cones', in four colours, made of PVC.
3.	Cricket stumps —	Spring release wicket, 71 cm high.
4.	Quoits, balls, hoops, bean bags —	Four colours and a full range of ball sizes.

The gymnastic equipment includes:

1.	4 Nesting agility tables — Blue frames, red vinyl top. Heights 62 cm, 76 cm, 91 cm and 107 cm.	
2.	Agility stool —	Blue frame, red vinyl top, height 91 cm.
3.	Tumbling mats —	61 cm x 183 cm, depth 5 cm in four colours, with Velcro fasteners to attach one mat to another — light and easy to move.
4.	Agility mat —	6ft x 4ft x 1in or 4ft x 3ft x 1in, in blue vinyl.
5.	Landing module —	8ft x 4ft x 10in, with a foam interior covered with rein-forced blue PVC. Rot-proof, anti-slip, can be used outdoors.

The special needs equipment includes:
Totally soft play environment (Design Centre Award) 17 different shapes available in four bright colours. Design services are available free. Also, probably the most comprehensive range of specially constructed balls, playrolls, barrels, rocking 'horses', punch balls and bop bags, flotation aids, tunnels, bikes, scooters, etc.

(The Special Education equipment has been given an award by the Physical Education Association of Great Britain and Northern Ireland.)

The nursery and reception class equipment includes:

Make your own! —	Giant toggle blocks. Combi kit. Quadro. Gymbo.
Turtle sandbox —	Turtle's shell forms a lid to protect the sand if stationed outdoors. Bright green PVC.
Oyster Shell —	Opens up to form two blue water troughs or sand trays. PVC.
Paddling Pool —	Can be assembled to a rigid structure.
Swing Seesaw Slide Roundabout Playcentre Joy-boat	Blue and red steel tube construction. Tough and moulded to resist outdoor weather conditions. Roundabout, joy-boat and playcentre can be used indoors.
Climbing frame and Scrambling net —	Two sizes: 160 cm x 160 cm and 254 cm x 182 cm.
'Hidey Hole' stairs 'Hidey Holes' Triangle and planks Multi-sit and ride	In polished plywood. Can be used together to create physical and imaginative experiences. Boxes with holes in, steps with holes in etc. Vehicle to ride.
Play tunnel	Galvanised spring wire covered in removable plastic cover.

Various scooters, tractors, trikes, cars, all sturdily constructed in heavy gauge materials.

New exciting apparatus includes:

An inflatable ball pool —	Can be used as a paddling pool.
Wombler —	Constructed for activity in strong polyurethene. Looks like a large ball cut in half, size 95 cm x 45 cm

SUPPLIERS OF NURSERY-OUTDOOR EQUIPMENT

Community Playthings, Robertsbridge, East Sussex TN32 5DR.
Nottingham Educational Supplies Ltd., 17 Ludlow Hill Road, West Bridgford, Nottingham NG2 6HD.

Hestair Hope Ltd., St. Phillips's Drive, Royston, Oldham, OL2 6AG.

Kimpan (UK) Ltd., 3 Holdon Avenue, Bletchley, Milton Keynes MK1 1QU.

Levercrest Ltd., Unit 3/2, Trinity Trading Estate, Sittingbourne, Kent ME10 2PW.

L. & M. Montrose Products Ltd., (CE3) 28–34 Fortress Road, London NW5 2JM

Record Playground Equipment, Beach Works, Canal Road, Selby, N. Yorks YO8 8AG.

Russell Leisure Products, Box 415, Roddinglaw, Gogar, Edinburgh EH12 9DW

Speelhout (UK) Ltd., Unit 5E, Fort Wallington Industrial Estate, Fareham, Hants PO16 8TT

SMP (Playgrounds) Ltd., Dept B85, Freepost, Chertsey, Surrey KT16 9BR.

Wicksteed Leisure, Digby Street, Kettering, Northamptonshire NN16 8YJ.

Index

toys 56
   water 180-1

water
   infant school 179-80
   pre-school 6, 68, 173-8
wet playtimes 23, 169-70